CALIFORNIA
DMV Written
TEST - DMV
Questions &
Answers - permit
test US-CA driver
handbook.

Welcome

ing: **DMV_Driving_Test**

ytb: **DMV Driving Test**

CALIFORNIA DMV Written TEST #1

the question 1. When driving in fog, rain, or snow, use:

1. Low beams.
2. High beams.
3. Fog lights only.

The correct answer is 1.

Low beam headlights should be used in fog, rain, and snow.

The light from high beams will reflect back to the driver
under these weather conditions,

causing a glare that will make it difficult to see ahead

the question 2. When you see this sign, you:

1. Are approaching a railroad crossing and should
prepare to stop.
2. Will always stop at the upcoming railroad crossing.
3. Should stop and wait for a signal before crossing
the railroad tracks.

The correct answer is 1.

This sign indicates that you are approaching a railroad crossing.

You must look, listen, slow down, and prepare to stop.

Wait for any trains to pass before you proceed.

the question 3. In which of the following scenarios should your wheels not be pointed straight ahead?

1. When waiting to make a left turn at a traffic light.
2. When parked on a hill or sloping driveway.
3. When parked on the side of a level roadway where there is no curb.

The correct answer is 2.

While waiting to turn left, keep your wheels pointed straight ahead until it is safe to start your turn.

If a vehicle hits you from behind,this will prevent you from veering into oncoming traffic.

When parked facing either uphill or downhill, turn the wheels so the vehicle will not roll into traffic if the brakes fail.

the question 4. You should increase the distance between your vehicle and the vehicle ahead when you:

1. Are following a small passenger vehicle.
2. Are being tailgated by another driver.
3. Are driving more slowly than the posted speed limit.

The correct answer is 2.

When being tailgated, create extra space in front of your vehicle and do not brake suddenly.

Slow down gradually or merge into another lane to prevent a collision with the tailgater.

the question 5. If a truck or bus is making a right turn where you also need to make a right turn, you should:

1. Quickly turn before the truck or bus is able to.
2. Wait until the truck or bus turns before you turn.
3. Squeeze between the truck or bus and the curb.

The correct answer is 2.

If you try to insert your vehicle between a turning truck or bus and a curb, you may suffer a serious crash.

To avoid a collision, do not turn until the truck or bus has completed its turn.

the question 6. When driving under snowy or icy conditions:

1. It is safe to use your cruise control.
2. Make speed and directional changes more gradually than you would otherwise.
3. Drive as you would under normal conditions.

The correct answer is 2.

When driving under snowy or icy conditions, you should make speed and directional changes gradually.

Never use cruise control when driving on snow or ice because your tires may lose contact with the road and you will lose control of your vehicle.

the question 7. Which of these statements is true about changing lanes?

1. You only need to turn and look over your right shoulder for lane changes to the right or left.
2. Look over your right shoulder for a right lane change and your left shoulder for a left lane change.
3. Vehicles with two outside mirrors do not have blind spots.

The correct answer is 2.

Before changing lanes, signal, look in all your mirrors, and look over your left or right shoulder to make sure the lane next to you is clear.

Looking over your shoulder is a way to check your blind spot to be sure there is no vehicle, motorcycle, or bicycle traffic in the next lane.

the question 8. If you approach a traffic light with a red signal and a police officer directs you to go through the intersection without stopping,
you should:

1. Stop until the light turns green.
2. Go through the intersection without stopping.
3. Come to a complete stop before proceeding.

The correct answer is 2.

Instructions given by police officers directing traffic always override posted traffic signals and signs.

Follow the officer's instructions.

the question 9. Which of the following factors affect an individual's absorption of alcohol?

1. Weight.
2. Height.
3. Intelligence.

The correct answer is 1.

Factors affecting a person's absorption of alcohol include the person's weight, their biological sex, the amount of food in their digestive tract, and the number of alcoholic beverages they have consumed.

The only thing to do to remove alcohol from a person's system is to wait.

the question 10. This white sign means:

1. You should slow down and move to the right lane.
2. Stay in the right lane if you are driving more slowly than other traffic.
3. Slower traffic must exit on the right.

The correct answer is 2.

A white, rectangular sign indicates that you must obey important rules.

This sign means that drivers should allow the left lane to remain open, when possible, for passing and for faster traffic.

the question 11. When being followed by a tailgater, which of the following will help you avoid being hit from behind?

1. Merging into another lane.
2. Decreasing your following distance.
3. Changing lanes frequently.

The correct answer is 1.

When being closely followed by a tailgater, you should slow down gradually or merge into another lane to prevent a collision with them.

the question 12. A broken yellow centerline means that:

1. Passing is not permitted.
2. Passing on the right is permitted when the way ahead is clear.
3. Passing on the left is permitted when the way ahead is clear.

The correct answer is 3.

A broken yellow centerline means that a driver may cross the centerline to pass another vehicle on the left as long as there is no oncoming traffic.

Drivers should never cross a solid yellow centerline in order to pass.

the question 13. You want to make a right turn at an upcoming intersection. You should slow down and:

1. Move toward the left side of your lane.
2. Avoid driving in the bicycle lane.
3. Signal for 100 feet before turning.

The correct answer is 3.

When making a right turn, you should begin signaling about 100 feet before the turn.

the question 14. Fatigue increases the risk of:

1. Missing an exit.
2. Being late for an appointment.
3. Falling asleep behind the wheel and crashing.

The correct answer is 3.

Fatigue causes errors related to speed and distance, increases your risk of being in a crash, and causes you to take more time to make decisions.

When you are fatigued, you could fall asleep behind the wheel and crash, injuring or killing yourself or others.

the question 15. An orange and red triangular sign on a vehicle always means:

1. The vehicle has the right-of-way.
2. Slow-moving vehicle.
3. Shoulder work ahead.

The correct answer is 2.

Slow-moving vehicles, such as farm tractors, road maintenance vehicles, and animal-drawn carts, display an orange and red triangle on the back.

the question 16. This sign means:

1. Cars on the right move first.
2. You have the right-of-way.
3. Let cross traffic pass before proceeding.

The correct answer is 3.

When approaching this sign, you must yield the right-of-way.

Slow down and let vehicles and pedestrians crossing your path pass before you proceed.

If necessary, stop before going ahead.

the question 17. Which of the following blocks the smooth flow of traffic?

1. Slowing down to look at collision scene.
2. Avoiding unnecessary lane changes.
3. Using public transportation instead of your vehicle.

The correct answer is 1.

Rubbernecking (the practice of slowing down to look at collisions or other out-of-the-ordinary things) contributes to traffic congestion and should be avoided.

the question 18. When driving in work zones, you should:

1. Increase your speed to get through the zone as quickly as possible.
2. Reduce your speed and be prepared to stop suddenly.
3. Maintain your normal speed the whole way through the zone.

The correct answer is 2.

When entering and driving through a work zone, slow down and be prepared to stop.

Obey posted speed limits and be alert to conditions around you. Workers could be present.

the question 19. When you are behind a motorcycle, you should:

1. Be ready to use your horn.
2. Drive more slowly.
3. Allow a larger following distance.

The correct answer is 3.

When following a motorcyclist, allow for at least a three- to four-second following distance.

Motorcycles can stop quickly and following them too closely endangers your life and that of the motorcyclist. If the motorcyclist should fall, you need extra distance to avoid the rider.

The chances of a fall are greatest on wet and icy roads, gravel roads, and metal surfaces such as bridges, gratings, and streetcar or railroad tracks.

the question 20. When backing up:

1. Look through the rear window.
2. Press hard on the gas pedal.
3. Rely only on your rearview mirror.

The correct answer is 1.

When backing up, place your right arm on the back of the passenger seat and look directly through the rear window.

Do not depend on your rearview or side mirrors as mirrors do not show directly behind your vehicle. Only drive in reverse at a low speed.

the question 21. When driving at night on a dimly lit street, you should:

1. rive slowly enough that you can stop within the area illuminated by your headlights.
2. Turn on your high beam headlights to better see the vehicles ahead of you.
3. Keep the instrument panel lights bright to be more visible to other drivers.

The correct answer is 1.

You should drive more slowly at night than during the day because it is not possible to see as far ahead at night.

You should make sure that you can stop within the area illuminated by your headlights.

the question 22. Which of these statements is true about drugs and driving?

1. Any prescription drug is safe to use if you don't feel drowsy.
2. Even over-the-counter drugs can impair your driving.
3. Only illegal drugs can impair your driving.

The correct answer is 2.

Legal prescription and over-the-counter drugs can impair your ability to drive, including drugs taken for colds, hay fever, allergies, or to calm nerves or muscles.

It is illegal to drive while under the influence of any drug that impairs your ability to drive safely; this law does not differentiate between illegal, prescription, or over-the-counter drugs.

the question 23. You are approaching an intersection at the posted speed limit when the signal turns yellow. You should:

1. Slow down and proceed through the intersection without caution.
2. Speed up to cross the intersection before the light turns red.
3. Stop before entering the intersection, if you can do so safely.

The correct answer is 3.

A solid yellow light means "caution" and signals that the light will soon turn red. You should stop at a solid yellow light if you can do so safely;

otherwise, you should cautiously cross the intersection.

the question 24. A person may legally ride in the back of a pickup truck when:
1. The sides of the pickup bed are at least 24 inches high.
2. The back of the pickup is covered with a camper shell.
3. In a secured seat and while using an approved safety belt.

The correct answer is 3.

Do not allow a person to ride in the back of a pickup or other truck unless the vehicle is equipped with seats and the person uses both the seat and a safety belt.

the question 25. You are approaching a green traffic light and traffic is blocking the intersection. What is the best thing to do?

1. Partially enter the intersection to establish your right-of-way.
2. Don't enter the intersection until you can get completely across.
3. Continue into the intersection and wait for traffic to clear.

The correct answer is 2.

Even if your light is green, you must not enter an intersection unless you can get completely through the intersection before the light turns red.

If you block the intersection, you can be cited.

the question 26. There are two traffic lanes moving in your direction. You are driving in the left lane and many vehicles are passing you on the right. If the driver behind you wishes to drive faster, you should:

1. Stay in your lane so you don't impede the flow of traffic.
2. Drive onto the left shoulder to let the other vehicles pass.
3. Move into the right lane when it is safe.

The correct answer is 3.

To drive quickly, pass, or turn left, use the left lane.

Use the right lane when driving more slowly than surrounding traffic, entering the road, or turning right.

the question 27. This sign means:

1. Yield the right-of-way.
2. No passing zone.
3. Reduction in lanes.

The correct answer is 1.

A triangular red and white sign indicates that you must yield the right-of-way.

the question 28. Yellow lines separate:

1. Traffic lanes on one-way streets.
2. Traffic moving in opposite directions on two-way roads.
3. All carpool lanes from regular traffic lanes.

The correct answer is 2.

Yellow lines mark the center of a road used for two-way traffic.

A solid yellow centerline indicates that drivers may not cross the line to pass.

A broken yellow centerline indicates that drivers may cross the line to pass, but only if passing would not interfere with traffic.

the question 29. When being passed by another vehicle:

1. Brake hard.
2. Maintain a constant speed.
3. Speed up.

The correct answer is 2.

When being passed, you must yield to the passing vehicle and not increase your speed. Allow the vehicle to safely merge back into your lane.

the question 30. This sign means:

1. Pedestrians walking along the road ahead.
2. Pedestrian crossing ahead.
3. Pedestrians must not cross here.

The correct answer is 2.

Warning signs are usually yellow with black markings.

If a pedestrian is crossing in a crosswalk marked with this sign, drivers must stop and remain stopped until the pedestrian is no longer in the crosswalk.

This sign alerts drivers to where pedestrians may be crossing.

the question 31. Drivers must use their seat belt:

1. Unless they are driving a vehicle built before 1978.
2. Unless they are driving a limousine.
3. And failure to do so will result in a traffic ticket.

The correct answer is 3.

Drivers must always wear seat belts and may be cited for failure to do so.

the question 32. If you are about to be hit from the rear, you should not:

1. Release your seat belt.
2. Brace yourself.
3. Press your head against the head restraint.

The correct answer is 1.

If your vehicle is hit from the rear while you are in forward motion, your body will be thrown backward.

Brace yourself by pressing against the back of your seat and putting your head against the head restraint to prevent whiplash.

Maintain a firm grip on the steering wheel and be ready to apply your brakes to avoid being pushed into another vehicle

the question 33. If you park facing uphill on a street with a curb, set the parking brake and:

1. Turn the front wheels toward the curb.
2. Turn the front wheels away from the curb.
3. Leave the front wheels straight.

The correct answer is 2.

When parking uphill on a road that has a curb, your wheels should be turned away from the curb.

When parking uphill on a street without a curb or when parking downhill, your wheels should be turned toward the curb or edge of the road.

the question 34. This sign means:

1. Side road.
2. Merge.
3. Yield the right-of-way.

The correct answer is 1.

This sign indicates that there is an intersection with a side road ahead.

the question 35. The driver ahead of you stops at a crosswalk. What should you do?

1. Cautiously pass the vehicle at 10 mph or slower.
2. Stop, proceeding only when all the pedestrians have crossed.
3. Change lanes, look carefully, and pass the stopped vehicle.

The correct answer is 2.

You must not pass a vehicle that is stopped at a crosswalk.

There may be pedestrians crossing the street that you cannot see. Instead, stop, proceeding only after all pedestrians have crossed.

the question 36. From top to bottom, the following is the proper order for traffic lights:

1. Red, yellow, green.
2. Red, green, yellow.
3. Green, red, yellow.

The correct answer is 1.

Warning signs are usually yellow with black markings.

They alert you to conditions that are immediately ahead. This sign warns drivers about the presence of traffic signals at an intersection ahead.

CALIFORNIA DMV Written TEST #2

the question 1. When you tailgate other drivers (drive closely to their rear bumper):

1. You can frustrate the other drivers and make them angry.
2. Your actions cannot result in a traffic citation.
3. You help reduce traffic congestion.

The correct answer is 1.

Most rear-end collisions are caused by tailgating. To avoid tailgating, use the "Three Second Rule." When the vehicle ahead of you passes a certain point, such as a sign, count "one-thousand-one, one-thousand-two, one-thousand-three." If you pass the same point before you finish counting, you are following too closely.

the question 2. Which child would require a child passenger restraint system?

1. A 9-year-old who is 4 feet 10 inches tall
2. A 10-year-old who is 5 feet 3 inches tall
3. A 7-year-old who is 4 feet 8 inches tall

The correct answer is 3.

Children who are eight years old or older, or who have reached at least 4 feet 9 inches in height, may use a properly secured safety belt meeting federal standards.

Other children must be seated in a child passenger restraint system.

the question 3. If you must park your vehicle in an area not usually used for parking:

1. Park with your reverse lights on.
2. Make sure your vehicle is visible to drivers approaching from any direction.
3. Park five feet from the curb.

The correct answer is 2.

Drivers are responsible for making sure their vehicles do not become hazards after they have been parked. Wherever you park, make sure your car is visible to drivers approaching from any direction.

the question 4. This sign means:

1. Do not enter.
2. Stop ahead.
3. Roadwork or maintenance is present.

The correct answer is 3.

Orange, diamond-shaped signs are used to mark construction, maintenance, survey, and utility work areas.

These signs help direct drivers and pedestrians safely through dangerous zones. Fines for traffic convictions may double in areas marked by these signs.

the question 5. Should you always drive more slowly than other traffic?

1. No, you can block traffic when you drive too slowly.
2. Yes, it is a good defensive driving technique.
3. Yes, it is always safer than driving faster than other traffic.

The correct answer is 1.

You must drive more slowly than usual when there is heavy traffic or bad weather.

However, if you block the normal and reasonable movement c traffic by driving too slowly, you may be cited.

the question 6. If your cell phone rings while you are driving and you do not have a hands-free device, you should:

1. Answer the call because it may be an emergency.
2. Let the call go to voicemail.
3. Check the incoming number before answering the call.

The correct answer is 2.

Drivers should not use a cell phone without a hands-free device.

For minors, it is illegal to use any cell phone while driving, except in an emergency.

Even if you do have a hands-free device, it is recommended that you let calls go to voicemail while driving in order to avoid distractions.

the question 7. Which of these statements is true about drinking alcohol and driving?

1. If you can walk in a straight line after drinking, it is safe to drive.
2. If you are under the legal blood alcohol concentration limit, your driving isn't impaired.
3. Alcohol affects judgement, which is needed to drive safely.

The correct answer is 3.

Being under the influence of alcohol affects your judgment.

Good judgement is necessary to react appropriately to things that you see or hear while on the road.

Even if you are below the legal blood alcohol limit, consuming any amount of alcohol is likely to affect your ability to drive safely.

the question 8. Unless otherwise posted, the speed limit in a residential area is:

1. 20 mph.
2. 25 mph.
3. 30 mph.

The correct answer is 2.

Unless otherwise posted, the speed limit in business and residential districts is 25 mph.

the question 9. When a school bus is stopped on the road ahead to load or unload children, you must:

1. Come to a complete stop until all the children have left the bus.
2. Come to a complete stop until the red lights stop flashing and the stop arm is withdrawn.
3. Change lanes, drive slowly, and pass the bus cautiously.

The correct answer is 2.

When a school bus is stopped on the road ahead with its lights flashing and its stop arm extended, you must come to a complete stop and wait to proceed until the lights have stopped flashing and the stop arm is withdrawn. Even after the bus begins to move again, do not proceed until you are sure there are no children crossing the road ahead of you.

the question 10. You must notify the DMV within five days if you:

1. Sell or transfer your vehicle.
2. Fail a smog test.
3. Get a new prescription for lenses or contacts.

The correct answer is 1.

If you sell or transfer a vehicle, you must report the sale or transfer to the DMV within five days.

the question 11. This sign means:

1. No left turn can be made here.
2. A left turn can be made only after stopping.
3. All traffic must turn right at the next intersection.

The correct answer is 1.

Signs with a red circle and diagonal line over a black symbol indicate that the action represented by the symbol is prohibited. In this case, the sign indicates that left turns are prohibited.

the question 12. This road sign means:

1. Intersection ahead.
2. Steep grade ahead.
3. Winding road.

The correct answer is 2.

Warning signs are usually yellow with black markings. This sign indicates that there is a steep hill ahead. Slow down and be ready to shift to a lower gear to control your speed and protect your brakes from damage.

the question 13. You may drive a motor vehicle in a bike lane:

1. If you drive more slowly than 15 mph.
2. No more than 200 feet before making a right turn.
3. Whenever bicyclists are not present.

The correct answer is 2.

If making a right turn, you may enter the bicycle lane no more than 200 feet before the corner or driveway.

Drivers of motor vehicles should not enter a bicycle lane at any other time.

the question 14. You are driving in the far right lane of a four-lane freeway and notice thick broken white lines on the left side of your lane. You are driving in:

1. The carpool lane and must merge into the next lane.
2. A special lane for slow-moving vehicles.
3. An exit lane.

The correct answer is 3.

Freeway lanes that are ending will usually be marked by large broken lines painted on the pavement.

If you are driving in a lane marked with these broken lines, be prepared to exit the freeway or for the lane to end.

the question 15. Vehicles stopped behind a school bus with its red lights flashing must remain stopped until :

1. All students are off the bus.
2. The stop arm is retracted.
3. The stop arm is retracted and the bus resumes motion.

The correct answer is 3.

When a school bus is flashing its red lights and has its stop arm extended, motorists must come to a full stop until the lights are turned off, the stop arm is withdrawn, and the bus begins moving again.

the question 16. If you drive more slowly than the flow of traffic, you will most likely:

1. Interfere with traffic and receive a ticket.
2. Improve traffic flow.
3. Demonstrate defensive driving techniques.

The correct answer is 1.

You must drive more slowly than usual when there is heavy traffic or bad weather.

However, if you block the normal and reasonable movement of traffic by driving too slowly, you may be cited.

You should match the speed of traffic, unless the speed of traffic exceeds the legal speed limit.

the question 17. This yellow sign means:

1. Controlled railroad ahead.
2. Be prepared to stop if the light is flashing.
3. There is a traffic signal ahead.

the question 18. You see a flashing yellow traffic signal at an upcoming intersection. The flashing yellow light means:

1. Stop before entering the intersection, as long as you can do so safely.
2. Stop. Yield to all cross traffic before crossing the intersection.
3. Slow down and cross the intersection carefully.

the question 19. Give the right-of-way to any pedestrian who is:

1. In a marked crosswalk.
2. In any crosswalk or intersection.
3. Crossing any street.

The correct answer is 3.

Drivers must yield the right-of-way to pedestrians who are crossing the street in any marked or unmarked crosswalk.

In the interest of safety, drivers should yield the right-of-way to people crossing any street.

the question 20. U-turns in residential districts are legal:

1. On a one-way street on a green arrow.
2. When there are no vehicles approaching nearby.
3. Across sets of solid double yellow lines.

The correct answer is 2.

U-turns are permitted in residential areas if there are no vehicles approaching within 200 feet.

They are also permitted when a traffic sign, light, or signal protects you from approaching vehicles.

the question 21. When driving on a multilane street with two-way traffic:

1. Drive alongside other vehicles so the drivers can see you.
2. You should drive ahead of or behind the other vehicles.
3. It is safest to drive in the lane next to the centerline.

The correct answer is 2.

Driving directly alongside another vehicle could create a collision if the other driver crowds your lane or tries to change lanes without looking.

To avoid this, you should drive ahead of or behind vehicles in other lanes rather than alongside them.

the question 22. You should allow an extra cushion of space:
1. When following a station wagon.
2. When following a driver who cannot see the rear of their vehicle.
3. When following a small passenger car.

The correct answer is 2.

Drivers of trucks, buses, vans, or any vehicles pulling campers or trailers may not be able to see you if you are driving directly behind them.

Increase your following distance when driving behind one of these vehicles. Additionally, large vehicles can block your view of the road, so increase your following distance to look around the sides of the vehicle and see the road ahead.

the question 23. California's "Basic Speed Law" says you must:

1. Keep your speed close to that of other traffic.
2. Never drive faster than is safe for current conditions.
3. Always drive at the posted speed limit.

The correct answer is 2.

The "Basic Speed Law" states that you may never drive faster than is safe for current conditions.

For example, if you drive at 45 mph in a 55 mph zone during a dense fog, even though you are below the posted limit, you may be cited for driving "too fast for conditions."

the question 24. This road sign means:

1. Intersection ahead.
2. Merging traffic.
3. Steep hill ahead.

The correct answer is 3.

Warning signs provide notice to road users of a situation that might not be readily apparent and are usually yellow with black markings. This sign warns drivers of an upcoming steep hill. Drivers should adjust their speed accordingly to avoid collisions and brake damage.

the question 25. You may cross a double yellow line to pass another vehicle if the yellow line next to:

1. The other side of the road is a solid line.
2. Your side of the road is a broken line.
3. The other side of the road is a broken line.

The correct answer is 2.

Double yellow lines in the center of the road indicate that you may pass if a broken line is next to your driving lane.

the question 26. This sign means:

1. Do not enter.
2. Yield the right-of-way.
3. Reserved parking for persons with disabilities.

The correct answer is 1.

This sign is posted on one-way streets and other roadways where a driver is not allowed to enter. A driver may see this sign if attempting to enter an expressway ramp in the wrong direction.

the question 27. This sign means:

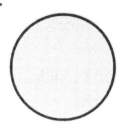

1. Railroad ahead.
2. No passing zone.
3. School zone.

The correct answer is 1.

A round yellow sign indicates that there is a railroad crossing ahead.

the question 28. If you encounter an aggressive driver, you should:

1. Challenge them.
2. Get out of their way.
3. Speed up.

The correct answer is 2.

Drivers must respect and cooperate with all other road users and conform to specific rules in order to maintain order and to avoid crashes. When encountering an aggressive driver, it is safest to just get out of their way.

Always avoid competing with other drivers.

the question 29. Which of these vehicles must always stop before crossing railroad tracks?

1. Tank trucks marked with hazardous materials placards.
2. Motor homes or pickup trucks towing a boat trailer.
3. Any vehicle with three or more axles and weighing more than 4,000 pounds.

The correct answer is 1.

Trucks transporting hazardous loads must stop before they cross railroad tracks.

the question 30. Water on the road can cause a vehicle to hydroplane. Your car may hydroplane at speeds as low as:

1. 45 miles per hour.
2. 35 miles per hour.
3. 40 miles per hour.

The correct answer is 2.

Hydroplaning occurs when there is standing water on a roadway. At speeds up to 35 mph, most tires will channel water away from the tire.

As your speed increases past 35 mph, tires cannot channel the water as well and your tires may start to lose contact with the road and ride over the water like a set of water skis.

the question 31. If you are convicted of driving with an excessive blood alcohol concentration (BAC), you may be sentenced to serve:

1. Up to six months in jail.
2. Up to 12 months in jail.
3. No jail time, but you must pay a fine of $500.

The correct answer is 1.

If you are convicted of DUI for the first time and you have an excessive BAC level, you may be sentenced to serve up to six months in jail and may be required to pay a fine between $390 and $1,000. Your vehicle may be impounded and is subject to storage fees.

the question 32. While driving, you should look 10 to 15 seconds ahead of you:

1. And focus on the middle of the road.
2. Because it is a legal requirement.
3. To see potential hazards early.

The correct answer is 3.

To avoid last-minute moves, scan the road 10 to 15 seconds ahead of your vehicle so you can see hazards early. Constantly staring at the road right in front of your vehicle is dangerous.

the question 33. You may not park your vehicle:

1. On the side of the freeway in an emergency.
2. Next to a red painted curb.
3. Within 100 feet of an elementary school.

The correct answer is 2.

No stopping, standing, or parking is permitted next to a red painted curb. However, buses may stop in a red curb zone marked for buses.

the question 34. To see vehicles in your blind spots, you should check:

1. The inside rearview mirror.
2. The outside rearview mirror.
3. Over your shoulders.

The correct answer is 3.

By definition, blind spots are areas that cannot be seen using your mirrors. To check your blind spots, you should look over your shoulders.

the question 35. This sign means:

1. No right turn.
2. Right turn on red light permitted with caution.
3. All traffic must turn right at next intersection.

The correct answer is 1.

Signs with a red circle and diagonal line over a black symbol indicate the action represented by the symbol is prohibited. In this case, the sign indicates that right turns are prohibited.

the question 36. If you have trouble seeing other vehicles because of dust or smoke blowing across the roadway, you should drive more slowly and turn on your:

1. Emergency flashers.
2. Parking lights.
3. Headlights.

The correct answer is 3.

You must turn on your headlights any time conditions prevent you from seeing other vehicles. Other drivers may have trouble seeing you, too.

CALIFORNIA DMV Written TEST #3

the question 1. Which of these statements is true about driving and taking medications?

1. Most cold medications can make a person drowsy.
2. Over-the-counter medications cannot impair driving ability if taken in the recommended dosages.
3. Medications are safe to take at any time, if prescribed by a doctor.

The correct answer is 1.

Remember that all medications, prescription or over-the-counter, are potentially dangerous and could impair your driving.

Over-the-counter medicines that you take for colds and allergies can make you drowsy and affect your driving ability.

It is your responsibility to know how your medication affects your ability to drive.

the question 2. When using a roundabout, drivers should:

1. Stop in the middle of the roundabout.
2. Yield to traffic already in the roundabout.
3. Yield to entering traffic.

The correct answer is 2.

A roundabout is a circular intersection that usually does not include a traffic signal and flows in a counterclockwise direction around a central island.

Motorists must enter from the right, yielding to traffic already in the roundabout, and follow the circle to the right until the desired roadway is reached.

the question 3. You may pass a vehicle when:

1. You are on a hill or curve.
2. You are on a road with a solid line next to your lane.
3. You are on a road with a broken line next to your lane.

the question 4. This sign shows one type of:

1. Right turn.
2. Intersection.
3. Lane change.

the question 5. As you approach an intersection with a flashing yellow light:

1. Stop before crossing the intersection.
2. Slow down and proceed with caution.
3. Wait for a green light before proceeding.

The correct answer is 2.

A flashing yellow light means that you should slow down, check for cross traffic, and proceed with caution.

the question 6. If your vehicle starts to lose traction because of water on the road, you should:

1. Drive at a constant speed to gain better traction.
2. Apply the brakes firmly to prevent your vehicle from sliding.
3. Slow down gradually and not apply the brakes.

The correct answer is 3.

When driving in heavy rain at speeds as low as 30 mph, your tires may lose all contact with the road and instead ride up on a layer of water above the surface of the road.

This is called "hydroplaning." If your vehicle starts to hydroplane, slow down gradually and do not apply the brakes.

the question 7. What is the difference between traffic lights with red arrows and those with solid red lights?

1. Red arrows are only used to stop traffic which is turning.
2. Red arrows are only used for protected turn lanes.
3. You cannot turn on a red arrow, even if you stop first

The correct answer is 3.

You may sometimes turn right when stopped by a solid red light. You may never turn left or right when stopped by a traffic light with a red arrow.

the question 8. It is illegal to park your vehicle:

1. In an unmarked crosswalk.
2. Within three feet of a private driveway.
3. In a bicycle lane.

The correct answer is 1.

It is illegal to park your car on a marked or unmarked crosswalk. You may park in a bicycle lane if there is not a "No parking" sign posted and your vehicle does not block a bicyclist..

the question 9. This sign means:

1. No right turn.
2. Stop sign ahead.
3. Divided highway.

The correct answer is 1.

This sign indicates that turns in the direction of the arrow (in this case, to the right) are prohibited.

the question 10. Extra space in front of a large truck is needed for:

1. Other drivers to merge onto the freeway.
2. The truck driver to stop the vehicle.
3. Other drivers when they want to slow down.

The correct answer is 2.

Because they are larger, trucks take longer to stop than cars traveling at the same speed. Other drivers should not pull in front of a truck and then slow down or stop.1

the question 11. You want to park uphill on a two-way road and there is no curb. Which direction do you turn your front wheels?

1. Straight ahead
2. Right, toward the side of the road
3. Left, toward the center of the road

The correct answer is 2.

When parking either uphill or downhill on a road that has no curb, you should turn your wheels so that the vehicle will roll away from the center of the road if the brakes fail.

the question 12. When entering the interstate, check for a gap in traffic in the nearest lane, adjust your speed to match traffic, signal, and:

1. Expect traffic to allow you to proceed into the lane, since you have the right-of-way.
2. Merge carefully into the gap.
3. Wait for the lane to clear before merging.

The correct answer is 2.

Before merging into interstate traffic, you should identify a gap, accelerate to the speed of traffic, and signal. Merge into the gap when it is safe to do so.

Be alert to other traffic and do not expect other drivers to clear the lane.

the question 13. If you are continually being passed on the right and the left while driving in the center lane of an expressway, you should:

1. Stay in the center lane.
2. Move to the lane on your right.
3. Move to the lane on your left.

The correct answer is 2.

If a road has four or more lanes with two-way traffic, drive in the right lanes unless you are passing or turning left. If you are on an interstate highway and are driving below the speed of the flow of traffic, use the right lane.

the question 14. On a multilane road, a dashed yellow line next to a solid yellow line means:

1. Passing is prohibited from both directions.
2. Passing is permitted from both directions.
3. Passing is permitted only from the direction next to the dashed line.

The correct answer is 3.

Where there are both solid and dashed yellow lines between lanes of traffic, only traffic directly next to the dashed line may cross the centerline to pass. Drivers next to the solid line may not pass.

the question 15. What should you do at an intersection with a flashing yellow signal light?

1. Maintain your speed but watch for other vehicles.
2. Stop before crossing the intersection.
3. Slow down and cross the intersection carefully.

The correct answer is 3.

Slow down and be alert before entering the intersection. Yield to any pedestrians, bicyclists, or vehicles in the intersection. You do not need to stop for a flashing yellow traffic signal light.

the question 16. Sudden wind gusts on highways:

1. Generally affect only the movement of large vehicle
2. Only cause visibility problems.
3. Can cause problems for all vehicles.

The correct answer is 3.

While it can create special problems for large vehicles, strong wind can cause problems for all drivers.

Wind can lower visibility by blowing dirt and dust into the roadway, but it can sometimes also physically move a vehicle.

the question 17. When passing another vehicle, you should return to your original lane when:

1. You can see both headlights of the passed vehicle in your rearview mirror.
2. You have cleared the front bumper of the passed vehicle.
3. You are 50 feet in front of the passed vehicle.

The correct answer is 1.

When passing another vehicle, move back into your original lane only when you can see the passed vehicle's headlights in your rearview mirror.

This ensures that you will have enough room to safely pull back in front of the other vehicle.

the question 18. Tailgating other drivers (driving too closely to their rear bumper):

1. Can frustrate other drivers and make them angry.
2. Cannot result in a traffic citation.
3. Reduces collisions by preventing being "cut off."

The correct answer is 1.

Tailgating is a common behavior that can lead to aggressive driving, and so it should be avoided. Drivers may face legal consequences for driving unsafely.

the question 19. When turning left at an intersection:

1. You should always yield to oncoming traffic and pedestrians.
2. Oncoming traffic and pedestrians should yield to you.
3. You should never yield to oncoming traffic and pedestrians.

The correct answer is 1.

When turning left at an intersection, yield the right-of-way to oncoming traffic and pedestrians. Once the intersection is clear and applicable signals allow, you may complete the turn.

the question 20. You should not start across an intersection if you know you will block the intersection when the light turns red:

1. Under any circumstances.
2. Unless you entered the intersection on a yellow light
3. Unless you entered the intersection on a green light.

The correct answer is 1.

Even if the signal is green, you must not enter an intersection unless you can get completely across before the light turns red. If you block the intersection, you can be cited.

the question 21. It is more dangerous to drive at night than during the day because:

1. You cannot see as far ahead at night.
2. The road is always more slippery at night.
3. Your reaction time is slower at night.

The correct answer is 1.

With decreased visibility and the glare of oncoming headlights, you cannot see as far ahead at night as you can during the day. Always use headlights and exercise caution when driving in the dark.

the question 22. When parking your vehicle on any hill:

1. One of your rear wheels should touch the curb.
2. Use your parking brake and leave the vehicle in "park."
3. Your front wheels should be parallel to the road, if there is no curb..

The correct answer is 2.

When parking on a hill, you should always leave your vehicle in gear or in the "park" position. If there is no curb, you should turn your front wheels so that the vehicle will roll away from the center of the road if the brakes fail.

If there is a curb, the front wheels should be turned toward it (if headed downhill) or away from and gently touching it (if headed uphill).

the question 23. Large trucks turning onto a street with two lanes in each direction:

1. May complete the turn in either of the two lanes.
2. Often have to use the left lane to complete the turn.
3. Must stay in the right lane at all times while turning.

The correct answer is 2.

Large trucks must often swing wide to complete a right turn.

A truck making a right turn may initially appear to be turning left because of the need to swing wide. When behind a turning truck, you should pay attention to the truck's turn signal to be aware of which way the trucker actually intends to turn.

the question 24. At dawn or dusk and in rain or snow, it can be hard to see and be seen. A good way to let other drivers know you are there is to turn:

1. Up the instrumental panel lights.
2. On your parking lights.
3. On your headlights.

The correct answer is 3.

You must use your headlights at any time when conditions prevent you from seeing other vehicles and when it may be difficult for other drivers to see you. Always use your low beam headlights if weather conditions require you to use your windshield wipers.

the question 25. This road sign means:

1. Cars in the right lane must slow down.
2. No left turn.
3. Merge.

The correct answer is 3.

Warning signs are usually yellow with black markings. This sign indicates that there could be traffic merging from the right, so drivers should prepare to allow traffic to safely merge.

the question 26. If you are being followed too closely on a two-lane road:

1. Reduce your speed slowly to encourage the tailgater to drive around you.
2. Speed up to increase the distance between you and the other car.
3. Apply your brakes to slow down, then resume your original speed.

The correct answer is 1.

If you are being followed too closely by another driver, merge into a different lane. If there is no lane available for merging, wait until the road ahead is clear and slowly reduce your speed.
This will encourage the tailgater to drive around you.

the question 27. A flashing yellow traffic signal at an intersection means:

1. You should treat the signal like a stop sign.
2. Stop. Yield to all cross traffic before crossing in the intersection.
3. Slow down and be alert at the upcoming intersection

The correct answer is 3.

A flashing yellow signal means "proceed with caution." You should slow down and be alert before entering the upcoming intersection and must yield to any pedestrians, bicycles, or vehicles in the intersection; however, you do not have to stop.

the question 28. This sign shows one type of:

1. Intersection.
2. Road curve.
3. Right turn.

The correct answer is 1.

Warning signs are usually yellow with black markings. They alert you to conditions that are immediately ahead. This sign warns drivers that another road crosses the highway ahead.

the question 29. Which lane must you be in before making a left turn from a one-way street?

1. The lane nearest the left curb.
2. The lane nearest the center of the street.
3. The lane nearest the right curb.

The correct answer is 1.

When making any turn, turn from the lane closest to the direction you wish to travel into the first available legal lane. If you are making a left turn from a one-way street, this means that you would make the turn from the lane nearest to the left curb.

the question 30. Stopping distances and the severity of collisions:

1. Decrease as a vehicle's speed increases.
2. Are not affected by a vehicle's speed.
3. Increase as a vehicle's speed increases.

The correct answer is 3.

Excessive vehicle speed can have disastrous effects. As a vehicle's speed increases, the potential impact of a collision also increases, elevating the possibility of serious injury and death.

Increase your following distance as your speed increases to ensure that you will be able to stop safely if needed.

the question 31. You are on the freeway and traffic is merging into your lane. You should:

1. Make room for the merging traffic, if possible.
2. Assert your right-of-way by driving faster.
3. Always maintain your position.

The correct answer is 1.

When traffic permits, you should make room to allow vehicles to merge into your lane.

the question 32. Blocking an intersection during "rush hour" traffic is not permitted:

1. Unless you entered the intersection on a green light.
2. Under any circumstances, even if your light is green.
3. Unless you have the right-of-way or a green light.

The correct answer is 2.

Even if your light is green, you should not enter an intersection unless you can get completely across before the light turns red. You can be cited if you block the intersection.

the question 33. The speed limit in any alley is:

1. 20 mph.
2. 15 mph.
3. 25 mph.

The correct answer is 2.
The speed limit in any alley is 15 mph. This is always the speed limit, whether or not it is posted.

the question 34. If you come to an intersection controlled by a flashing yellow light, you must:

1. Wait for the green light before proceeding.
2. Slow down and cross the intersection carefully.
3. Stop before crossing the intersection.

The correct answer is 2.
A flashing yellow traffic light means drivers must slow down, be more aware, and proceed with caution. Be alert to crossing traffic and pedestrians.

the question 35. On a freeway, you should look farther ahead than you would on a city street:

1. In order to see potential hazards early.
2. Because it takes a quarter of a mile to stop your vehicle completely.
3. Because it helps you keep up with traffic.

The correct answer is 1.

On the freeway, be ready for changes in traffic conditions. Watch for signals from other drivers. Expect merging vehicles at on-ramps and interchanges and be prepared for rapid changes in road conditions and traffic flow.

the question 36. At an uncontrolled intersection where you cannot see cross traffic until you are just about to enter the intersection, the speed limit is:

1. 15 mph.
2. 25 mph.
3. 20 mph.

The correct answer is 1.

The speed limit for a blind intersection is 15 mph. An intersection is considered "blind" if there are no stop signs on any corner and you cannot see for 100 feet in either direction during the last 100 feet before crossing.

CALIFORNIA DMV Written TEST #4

the question 1. Before you change lanes, you should check your mirrors and:

1. Never look over your right shoulder.
2. Always slow down in your traffic lane.
3. Glance over your shoulder.

The correct answer is 3.

Before changing lanes, it is very important to check behind you. You should look over your shoulder to ensure that you are not getting in the way of vehicles in the lane you want to enter

Before changing lanes, you should also ensure that no drivers are attempting to drive into the same spot from a different lane.

the question 2. Dim your headlights for oncoming vehicles or when you are within 300 feet of a vehicle:

1. That you are approaching from behind.
2. Approaching you from behind.
3. That you have already passed.

The correct answer is 1.

You are required to dim your headlights to low beams within 500 feet of a vehicle that is coming toward you and within 300 feet of a vehicle that you are following.

the question 3. You can drive off the road to pass another vehicle:

1. If the vehicle ahead is turning left.
2. If there are two or more lanes traveling in your direction.
3. Under no circumstances.

The correct answer is 3.

You may never drive off the paved or main-traveled portion of the road and onto the shoulder to pass another vehicle.

the question 4. Using a cell phone while operating a motor vehicle is considered a distraction because:

1. It causes the driver to be concerned about the cost of the call.
2. It occupies the driver's hands, eyes, and mind.
3. It is an activity that draws the attention of other drivers.

The correct answer is 2.

Using a cell phone while driving is dangerous because it occupies the user's eyes, hands, and mind. Even the most skilled drivers increase their risk of being involved in a crash by using a cell phone on the road.

the question 5. Alcohol is:

1. A stimulant.
2. An antihistamine.
3. A depressant.

The correct answer is 3.

Alcohol is a depressant that dulls your judgment and makes your reflexes unreliable.

the question 6. Excessive speed:

1. Does not increase the chance of a crash.
2. Increases your ability to react to a hazard.
3. Often leads to high-risk decision-making.

The correct answer is 3.

Excessive speed is one of the most common contributing factors to vehicle crashes. Excessive speed does not save time and often leads to high-risk decision-making.

the question 7. A distraction when driving is:

1. Anything that causes evasive action while driving.
2. Anything that takes your attention away from driving.
3. Anything that causes you to pay more attention to driving.

The correct answer is 2.

A distraction when driving is anything that takes your attention away from driving. Driver distractions may occur anytime and anywhere. Distracted driving can cause collisions, resulting in property damage, injury, and death.

the question 8. Smoking inside a vehicle with a person younger than 18 years of age is:

1. Legal, if it is your child.
2. Illegal at all times.
3. Not restricted by law.

The correct answer is 2.

In California, it is illegal to smoke in a vehicle at any time when a minor is present.

the question 9. You must notify the DMV within five days if you:

1. Are cited for a traffic violation.
2. Sell or transfer your vehicle.
3. Paint your vehicle a different color.

The correct answer is 2.

You are required by law to contact the DMV within five calendar days from the date you sell or transfer the title of a vehicle to another owner. They must be notified of every title transfer.

the question 10. You are driving on the freeway behind a large truck. You should drive:

1. Closer behind the truck than you would if following a passenger vehicle.
2. Farther behind the truck than you would if following a passenger vehicle.
3. To the right side of the truck and wait to pass.

The correct answer is 2.

It is necessary to follow farther behind a large truck than you would if following a passenger vehicle because trucks have larger blind spots.

the question 11. This white sign means:

1. The railroad crossing is controlled. Continue at your regular speed.
2. Look, listen, and prepare to stop at the crossing if necessary.
3. Stop at the railroad tracks and wait for a signal before crossing.

The correct answer is 2.

When approaching a railroad crossing, you must look, listen, slow down, and prepare to stop. Let any trains pass before you proceed.

the question 12. Increase your following distance when driving behind a large vehicle:

1. To better see around the sides of the vehicle.
2. Because other drivers tend to pull behind large vehicles before trying to pass them.
3. Because following too closely will get you caught in the vehicle's slipstream.

The correct answer is 1.

Drivers of trucks, buses, vans, and any vehicles pulling campers or trailers may not be able to see you if you are driving directly behind them. Increase your following distance when driving behind one of these vehicles. Additionally, large vehicles can block your view of the road, so increase your following distance to look around the sides of the vehicle and see the road ahead.

the question 13. What is an important step in turning?

1. Check traffic in all directions.
2. Increase your speed.
3. Always move to the left lane.

The correct answer is 1.

When turning, you should look to the rear and both sides of your vehicle to ensure it is safe to proceed before making the turn. Adjust your speed to safely complete the turn.

the question 14. If you miss your exit on the freeway, you should not:

1. Continue on the freeway and find an alternate route to your destination.
2. Proceed to the next exit, leave the freeway, and return to your proper exit.
3. Back up on the road or shoulder.

The correct answer is 3.

If you miss your turn or exit, do not back up in the travel lane or on the shoulder. Continue to drive to the next exit or crossroad.

Drivers do not expect a vehicle to be backing toward them or the roadway and doing so will likely cause a collision.

the question 15. Adjust your rearview and side mirrors:

1. Before you start driving.
2. Whenever you need to use them.
3. Before you get into the car.

The correct answer is 1.

Your safety and the safety of other drivers and pedestrians depends a lot on what you do before driving. Before moving your vehicle, you should adjust your seat, adjust your mirrors, fasten your safety belt, and secure items in and on your vehicle. Do not wait until your vehicle is moving to adjust your mirrors.

the question 16. Which of the following driving skills is/are affected by the use of alcohol and/or drugs?

1. Alertness.
2. Coordination.
3. Both of the above.

The correct answer is 3.

Alcohol and other drugs can negatively effect a number of skills needed for safe driving, including a driver's reaction time, coordination, alertness, and ability to concentrate.

the question 17. Night driving presents unique problems because:

1. The speed limit is increased at night.
2. There are fewer cars on the roads at night.
3. Distance and vehicle speed are difficult to judge in the dark.

The correct answer is 3.

Night driving creates a unique set of problems for drivers.

Due to the reduced visibility, it can be difficult to judge distance and the traveling speeds of other vehicles when driving at night. Drivers can see only as far as their headlights allow.

the question 18. A pedestrian starts to cross the street after the "Don't Walk" signal begins to flash. The pedestrian is in the middle of the street when your signal light changes to green. You should:

1. Proceed if you have the right-of-way.
2. Proceed if the pedestrian is not in your lane.
3. Wait until the pedestrian crosses the street before proceeding.

The correct answer is 3.

At a green light, you must give the right-of-way to any vehicle, bicyclist, or pedestrian in the intersection.

If a pedestrian begins crossing the street after the traffic signal light starts flashing, wait until they have crossed the street before proceeding.

the question 19. You are approaching an intersection where a traffic signal is displaying a steady yellow light. If you have not already entered the intersection, you should:

1. Speed up to beat the red light.
2. Reduce you speed and proceed carefully through the intersection.
3. Come to a safe stop.

The correct answer is 3.

At an intersection controlled by a steady yellow light, you should bring your vehicle to a safe stop. If you are already within the intersection when the light changes from green to yellow, continue through the intersection at a safe speed.

the question 20. When changing lanes on a freeway, you should:

1. Signal for at least five seconds.
2. Slow down before you start to change lanes.
3. Assume there is enough space in the next lane for your vehicle, if you signal first.

The correct answer is 1.

Signal at least five seconds prior to a changing lanes on a freeway. Always signal when turning left or right, changing lanes, slowing down, or stopping to let other drivers, motorcyclists, bicyclists, and pedestrians know your intentions.

the question 21. Always carefully look for motorcycles before you change lanes because:

1. Their small size can make them hard to see.
2. They usually have the right-of-way at intersections.
3. It is illegal for motorcycles to share traffic lanes.

The correct answer is 1.

You should check carefully for motorcycles when changing lanes because their small size makes it easy for them to disappear into your blind spots.

the question 22. If you are driving on a highway next to a single broken white line marking:

1. You cannot cross the line to pass.
2. You may cross the line to pass and change lanes.
3. You may only cross the line to change lanes if you are in the left lane.

The correct answer is 2.

White lines separate lanes of traffic moving in the same direction. You may cross a dashed white line to pass or change lanes if it is safe to do so.

the question 23. The safest precaution that you can take when using cellular phones while driving is:

1. To use hands-free devices so you can keep both hands on the steering wheel.
2. To keep your phone within easy reach so you won't need to take your eyes off the road.
3. To review the number before answering a call.

The correct answer is 1.

Minors may not use a cellular phone while driving, except for certain emergencies. Cell phones are allowed to be used by drivers over age 18, but a hands-free device should be used.

the question 24. If a child is riding a bicycle near your vehicle:

1. Beep your horn.
2. Expect the child to be in total control of the bicycle.
3. Expect the unexpected.

The correct answer is 3.

Children on bicycles are sometimes unpredictable. Young bicyclists are especially likely to make surprising changes in direction. Remember that children and bicycles are both small in stature and may become difficult to see.

the question 25. A blood alcohol concentration of 0.02 percent:

1. Won't have any effect on your driving.
2. Won't put other drivers at risk.
3. Will double your chances of having an accident.

The correct answer is 3.

Every 0.02 percent increase in blood alcohol concentration nearly doubles a driver's risk of being in a fatal crash.

the question 26. A broken yellow line between two lanes of traffic means:

1. Both lanes of traffic are going in the same direction.
2. Passing is permitted when it's safe.
3. Passing is not permitted.

The correct answer is 2.

Dashed yellow lines separate single lanes of traffic moving in opposite directions. Passing is allowed when there is no oncoming traffic in the passing lane.

the question 27. When parking next to a curb, you should use your turn signals:

1. Only when pulling away from the curb.
2. When pulling next to, but not away from, the curb.
3. When pulling next to or away from the curb.

The correct answer is 3.

Drivers should signal when pulling next to a curb or away from a curb.

the question 28. You are driving on the freeway. The vehicle in front of you is a large truck. You should drive:

1.   Closely behind the truck in bad weather because the driver can see farther ahead than you can.
2. Farther behind the truck than you would when following a passenger vehicle.
3. No more than one car length behind the truck so the driver can see you.

The correct answer is 2.

When you follow so closely behind a truck that you cannot see the truck driver's side view mirrors, the trucker cannot see you and has no way of knowing you are there.

Tailgating a truck, or any vehicle, is dangerous because you take away your own cushion of safety if the vehicle in front of you stops quickly.

the question 29. A pentagon-shaped sign is a:

1. Stop sign.
2. Regulatory sign.
3. School zone or school crossing sign.

The correct answer is 3.

A five-sided sign is used to alert drivers to a school zone. Some pentagonal signs specifically indicate crosswalks within school zones where children or other pedestrians may be present.

the question 30. If oncoming headlights are blinding you while you are driving at night, you should:

1. Look toward the right edge of the road.
2. Switch your lights to high beams.
3. Turn your lights on and off.

The correct answer is 1.

If the headlights of an oncoming vehicle are blinding, glance toward the right edge of the road instead of looking directly ahead. This should keep your vehicle safely on the road until you pass the oncoming vehicle.

the question 31. It is illegal to leave a child age _____ or younger alone in a vehicle.

1. Eight
2. Seven
3. Six

The correct answer is 3.

It is never a good idea to leave a child unattended in a car. It is illegal to leave a child who is age six or younger unattended in a vehicle. A child may be left in a car if they are under the supervision of a person age 12 or older.

the question 32. You have stopped for a train at a railroad crossing. After the train passes, you should:

1. Wait for signal lights to stop flashing.
2. Look for a second train.
3. Both of the above.

The correct answer is 3.

Even after a train passes, watch out for a second train approaching on any track. Do not proceed until all gates have been lifted and all warning signals have stopped flashing.

the question 33. When you want to change lanes, you should never:

1. Move into another lane while within an intersection.
2. Check your blind spot by looking over your shoulder.
3. Check for other drivers moving into the same lane.

The correct answer is 1.

You should never change lanes within an intersection. Before changing lanes, always look over your shoulder to check your blind spot. Be alert to other drivers moving into the same lane.

the question 34. It is very foggy. You should slow down and:

1. Turn on your emergency flashers.
2. Turn your lights to their high beam setting.
3. Turn your lights to their low beam setting.

The correct answer is 3.

Use your low beams when driving in fog, snow, rain, or mist. Light from high beams will reflect off of precipitation, causing a glare and making it even more difficult to see.

Some vehicles are equipped with fog lights that should be used in addition to low beam headlights.

the question 35. If you want to pass a bicyclists riding on the right edge of your lane:

1. You must honk your horn before passing the bicyclist.
2. You must not squeeze past the bicyclist.
3. You may not pass the bicyclist for any reason.

The correct answer is 2.
When passing a bicyclist, you must allow at least three feet of space between your vehicle and the bicycle whenever possible. You must not squeeze the bicyclist off the road.

the question 36. After passing a vehicle, it is safe to return to your driving lane when:

1. The driver you passed signals for you to return to your lane.
2. You signal your intention for three seconds.
3. You see the headlights of the passed vehicle in your rearview mirror.

The correct answer is 3.
Before you return to your driving lane, be sure you are not dangerously close to the vehicle you have just passed. One way to do this is to look for the vehicle in your inside rearview mirror.
When you can see both headlights in your rearview mirror, you may have enough room to return to your driving lane.

CALIFORNIA DMV Written TEST #5

the question 1. The amount of alcohol in the blood is referred to as:

1. Implied consent (IC).
2. Blood alcohol concentration (BAC).
3. Rate of alcohol consumption (RAC).

The correct answer is 2.
Blood alcohol concentration (BAC) is a measurement of the percentage of alcohol in the blood. The higher the BAC number, the more impaired a person is.

the question 2. At a red traffic light with a green arrow, you may proceed in the direction of the arrow if:

1. You first come to a complete stop.
2. You wait until the light changes.
3. You are in the proper lane and the roadway is clear.

The correct answer is 3.
If you are in a lane corresponding to a signal displaying a green arrow, you may proceed in the direction of the arrow when the way is clear. This is true whether the arrow is displayed alone or together with another signal.

the question 3. Safely backing your vehicle requires all of the following, except:

1. Looking over your right shoulder as you back up.
2. Checking your vehicle's surroundings.
3. Tapping your horn before you back up.

The correct answer is 3.

Backing up is always dangerous because it is hard to see behind your vehicle. Prior to entering your vehicle, check your surroundings to be aware of any potential hazards.

When you are backing out of a parking space, look over your shoulder to maintain awareness of your surroundings.

the question 4. To turn left from a multilane one-way street onto a one-way street, you should start your turn from:

1. Any lane (as long as it is safe).
2. The lane closest to the left curb.
3. The lane in the center of the road.

The correct answer is 2.

When turning left from a one-way street onto another one-way street, you should begin the turn from the far left lane.

the question 5. For which of the following traffic lights must you always stop your vehicle?

1. Solid red lights, flashing red lights, and blacked out traffic signals.
2. Solid red lights, red arrows, and flashing yellow lights.
3. Solid red lights, flashing red lights, and yellow lights.

The correct answer is 1.

You must stop at a solid or flashing red light, or at a signal light that is blacked out (not working). A solid yellow light means that the signal is about to turn red and you must stop if you can do so safely; otherwise, proceed cautiously.

A flashing yellow light means that you should proceed with caution, but you do not need to stop.

the question 6. With a Class C driver license, a person may drive:

1.   A three-axle vehicle if the Gross Vehicle Weight is less than 6,000 pounds.
2. Any three-axle vehicle, regardless of the weight.
3. A vehicle pulling two trailers.

The correct answer is 1.

A person with a Class C license may drive a three-axle vehicle if it weighs 6,000 pounds or less.

the question 7. You must yield to a pedestrian using a white cane or guide dog:

1. Only when the guide dog is leading the person across the street.
2. At all times.
3. Only if a crossing guard is present.

The correct answer is 2.

Pedestrians who use guide dogs or white canes (with or without a red tip) must be given the right-of-way at all times.

the question 8. This yellow signs means:

1. The road ahead has many curves.
2. There is a sharp curve in the road ahead.
3. The road ahead may be slippery.

The correct answer is 3.

This sign indicates that the road ahead may be slippery when wet.

the question 9. Always use your seat belt:

1. Unless the vehicle was built before 1978.
2. Unless you are in a limousine.
3. When the vehicle is equipped with seat belts.

The correct answer is 3.

Use of seat belts is required for the driver and all passengers, including children who are over 8 years old or are at least 4 feet 9 inches tall. You must wear seat belts and shoulder harnesses even if the vehicle has airbags. If your vehicle is equipped with separate lap and shoulder belts, you must use both.

the question 10. This sign means:

1. Winding road ahead.
2. Do not enter.
3. Pedestrian crossing.

The correct answer is 1.
This sign warns of a winding road ahead.

the question 11. Roads are slippery after it first starts to rain. When the road is slippery, you should:

1. Avoid making turns and stops while driving at high speeds.
2. Test your tires' traction while going uphill.
3. Decrease the distance you look ahead of your vehicle.

The correct answer is 1.

A wet, slippery road does not allow your tires the traction they need, so it is necessary to drive more slowly on a wet road than you would on a dry road. To reduce the risk of skidding, you should avoid fast turns or stops.

the question 12. This road sign means:

1. Do not enter.
2. Roundabout ahead.
3. No U-turns.

The correct answer is 3.

Regulatory signs provide notice to road users of traffic laws that must be obeyed. This sign tells drivers that it is prohibited to make a U-turn.

the question 13. To improve visibility lowered by rain or fog, drivers should use their:

1. Low beam headlights.
2. High beam headlights.
3. Parking lights.

The correct answer is 1.

Low beam headlights should be used when driving in rainy or foggy weather. Even if they do little to help you see, low beams will make it easier for others to see you.

the question 14. Two sets of solid double yellow lines that are two or more feet apart:

1. May be crossed to enter or exit a private driveway.
2. May not be crossed for any reason.
3. Should be treated as a separate traffic lane.

The correct answer is 2.

Two sets of solid double yellow lines spaced two or more feet apart are considered a barrier. You may not drive on or over this barrier, or make a left turn or U-turn across it, except at designated openings.

the question 15. In rainy weather, you should be most careful when turning or stopping:

1. After it has been raining all day.
2. One half hour after it stops raining.
3. During the first half hour of rain.

The correct answer is 3.

You should be extra careful when turning and stopping during the first half hour of rain. At this point, the oil from cars has not yet washed off the pavement and could be forming a slippery mixture with the rain.

the question 16. When passing another vehicle, it is safe to return to your lane if you:

1. Cannot see the vehicle directly to your right.
2. See the vehicle's headlights in your rearview mirror.
3. Have passed the other vehicle's front bumper.

The correct answer is 2.

Before returning to your original lane after passing, you must make sure you are not dangerously close to the vehicle you have just passed.

When you can see both of the vehicle's headlights in your rearview mirror, you may have enough room to return to the lane.

the question 17. This road sign means:

1. Sharp right turn ahead.
2. A road joins from the right.
3. The road ahead turns sharply right then sharply left.

The correct answer is 3.

Warning signs are usually yellow with black markings. This sign indicates that the road ahead will turn sharply to the right and then sharply to the left.

the question 18. If you come to an intersection and your view to the side is blocked, you should:

1. Slow down and look both ways.
2. Maintain your speed and look both ways.
3. Stop, then inch forward until you can see clearly in both directions.

The correct answer is 3.

Drivers must slow down when approaching an intersection. If a clear view of cross traffic is obscured, a driver should come to a stop and inch forward until they can see clearly in both directions.

the question 19. It is legal to drive with an alcoholic beverage container that has been opened only if the container is:

1. Under the front seat.
2. In the glove department.
3. In the trunk.

The correct answer is 3.

Any opened alcoholic beverage container must be kept in the trunk of the vehicle, or in another place where passengers do not sit. Keeping an opened alcoholic drink in the glove compartment is specifically prohibited. However, in a bus, taxi, camper, or motor home, these restrictions do not apply to non-driving passengers.

the question 20. When driving in work zones, you should:

1. Follow the driver in front of you closely.
2. Pass the driver in front of you as soon as you can.
3. Avoid tailgating and keep a safe following distance.

The correct answer is 3.

When driving in a work zone, keep a safe distance between your vehicle and traffic barriers, trucks, construction equipment, workers, and other vehicles. Increase your following distance and do not tailgate.

the question 21. You should not use your horn:

1. When visibility ahead is limited.
2. If you might hit another vehicle.
3. Near blind pedestrians.

The correct answer is 3.
When driving near a blind pedestrian, using your horn may
be dangerous. Yield to the pedestrian and proceed when
it is safe to do so.

the question 22. Which of these statements is true
about roadwork zones?

1. Fines are the same for violations committed in work
zones as they are under normal traffic conditions.
2. You must "Slow for the Cone Zone".
3. Slow down only if you think workers are present.

The correct answer is 2.
Reduce your speed and be prepared to slow down or stop for
highway equipment. Driving carefully through work zones
improves safety for drivers, pedestrians, bicyclists, and road
workers.

the question 23. You are driving on a city street and see an emergency vehicle with flashing lights behind you. What should you do?

1. Drive to the right edge of the road and slow down.
2. Drive to the right edge of the road and stop.
3. Stay in your lane, slow down, and let it pass.

The correct answer is 2.

You must yield the right-of-way to any emergency vehicle that is using its siren and lights. Drive to the right edge of the road and stop until the emergency vehicle has passed.

If you are within an intersection, drive through the intersection first and then stop.

the question 24. When passing on the left of a vehicle it is safe to move back into the right lane:

1. After about three seconds.
2. When you can no longer see the vehicle over your right shoulder.
3. When you can see the front of the vehicle in your rearview mirror.

The correct answer is 3.

When passing another vehicle on its left, you may move back into the right lane when the headlights of the passed vehicle can be seen in your rearview mirror. Always signal before changing lanes.

the question 25. Which of the following roadways freeze first when wet?

1. Bridges and overpasses.
2. Intersections.
3. Tunnels.

The correct answer is 1.
Bridges and overpasses tend to freeze before the rest of the road does.

the question 26. When driving in fog or mist, never put your headlights on the high beam setting because:

1. The light will reflect back into your eyes.
2. Approaching vehicles might not see you.
3. Vehicles behind you may follow too closely.

The correct answer is 1.
In foggy or misty conditions, you should not use your headlights on their high beam setting because the light will be reflected back into your eyes.

the question 27. To turn left from a one-way street onto a one-way street, start from:

1. The lane closest to the left curb.
2. The center lane.
3. Any lane, as long as it seems safe to do so.

The correct answer is 1.

When turning left from a one-way street onto a one-way street, start the turn from the far left lane.

Watch for pedestrians, motorcyclists, and bicyclists between your vehicle and the curb because they may also legally use the left turn lane for their left turns. Turn into any lane that is safely open.

the question 28. If you find yourself in a skid:

1. Brake lightly.
2. Stay off the brakes.
3. Brake abruptly.

The correct answer is 2.

If your vehicle begins to skid, do not use the brakes. Braking could make the skid worse.

the question 29. If you see orange construction signs and cones on a freeway, you must:

1. Slow down because the lane ends ahead.
2. Be prepared for workers and equipment ahead.
3. Change lanes and maintain your current speed.

The correct answer is 2.

As you enter a work zone, signs and message boards will warn you of workers, slow-moving equipment, and/or closed lanes ahead. You should reduce your speed and be prepared to slow down or stop.

the question 30. Before switching on the ignition, you should:

1. Buckle your safety belt.
2. Be sure all passengers have buckled their safety belts.
3. Both of the above.

The correct answer is 3.

Develop a routine for entering and leaving your car. Before switching on the ignition, buckle your safety belt and see that all passengers do likewise.

the question 31. When turning left from a two-way street onto a one-way street, you should:

1. Turn into any lane.
2. Turn into first lane.
3. Turn into second lane.

The correct answer is 2.

When making any turn, turn from the lane closest to the direction you wish to travel into the first available legal lane. On a turn from a two-way to a one-way street, this means you should turn into the first lane.

the question 32. This sign means:

1. Stop sign ahead.
2. Railroad crossing ahead.
3. Construction ahead.

The correct answer is 2.

A round sign always indicates that you are approaching a railroad crossing.

the question 33. Which of the following is not a safe driving practice when driving on the interstate?

1. Slower traffic must keep to the right.
2. Change lanes without signaling.
3. If you miss your exit, you must go to the next exit.

The correct answer is 2.

You should always signal when moving your vehicle to the right or left. On an interstate, you should stay in the right lane if you are moving more slowly than the surrounding traffic.

It is illegal to back up or make a U-turn on interstate highways, so if you miss your exit, you should proceed to the next exit.

The question 34. You exit the freeway on a ramp that curves downhill. You should:

1. Slow to a safe speed before the curve.
2. Slow to the posted speed limit for the freeway.
3. Wait until you have entered the curve to begin braking.

The correct answer is 1.

You should always slow down before entering a curve. You may not be able to see hazards ahead and braking in a curve may cause your vehicle to skid.

the question 35. Which of these is a safe driving technique?

1. Using your high beam lights in the fog.
2. Staring at the road ahead of your vehicle.
3. Checking your rearview mirrors frequently.

The correct answer is 3.

To stay aware of hazards, you should scan the road and check your rearview mirrors every two to five seconds. Constantly staring at just the road ahead of you is dangerous. If you must drive in foggy conditions, you should use your low beam headlights, not your high beam headlights.

the question 36. You should always travel:

1. At the speed of vehicles surrounding you.
2. At the speed limit.
3. At a speed appropriate for road and weather conditions.

The correct answer is 3.

The speed at which you should drive your vehicle depends on road conditions, the weather, and the legal speed limit. You may never drive above the legal speed limit. Decrease your speed when anything makes conditions less than ideal.

CALIFORNIA DMV Written TEST #6

the question 1. This sign means:

1. All traffic must turn left.
2. No left turn.
3. No U-turn.

the question 2. Which of the following statements about blind spots is true?

1. They are eliminated if you have one outside mirror on each side of the vehicle.
2. Large trucks have bigger blind spots than most passenger vehicles.
3. Blind spots can be checked by looking in your rearview mirrors.

the question 3. If you are driving and you see animals standing near the roadway:

1. Speed up to scare them away.
2. Slow down and proceed with caution.
3. Quickly swerve into the next lane.

The correct answer is 2.

Slow down and proceed with caution if you see animals that are standing near the roadway. They may unexpectedly bolt or change direction at the last moment. Some animals travel in packs, so there may be more animals just out of sight that are also near the road.

the question 4. You should yield to a pedestrian:

1. Only if they are in a crosswalk.
2. At all times, even if the pedestrian is not obeying traffic laws.
3. Only if the traffic lights are in the pedestrian's favor.

The correct answer is 2.

Always be aware of pedestrians near your vehicle. You must do everything you can to prevent striking a pedestrian, regardless of the circumstances.

the question 5. When planning to pass another vehicle, you should:

1. Not count on other drivers to make room for you.
2. Assume the driver will let you pass if you use your turn signal.
3. Assume the driver will maintain a constant speed.

The correct answer is 1.

When planning to pass, do not count on having enough time to pass several vehicles at once or assume that other drivers will make room for you. When you can see both headlights of the passed vehicle in your rearview mirror, you may have enough room to return to your driving lane.

the question 6. You hit a parked vehicle and can't find the owner. What must you do?

1. Call your insurance company when you get home.
2. Wait for the owner to return.
3. Leave a note with your name and address on the parked vehicle.

The correct answer is 3.

If you hit a parked vehicle or other property, you must leave a note with your name, phone number, and address securely attached to the vehicle or property that you hit.

the question 7. If you plan to pass another vehicle, you should:

1. Not assume the other driver will make space for you to return to your lane.
2. Assume the other driver will let you pass if you use your turn signal.
3. Assume the other driver will maintain a constant speed.

The correct answer is 1.
Even when you signal, you should not assume that the space you want to occupy is free or that other drivers will give you the right-of-way.

he question 8. This sign means:

1. Merge.
2. Winding road ahead.
3. Reserved parking for persons with disabilities.

The correct answer is 1.
This sign warns that two lanes of traffic going the same direction will soon merge into one lane.

the question 9. A broken yellow centerline indicates that:
1. Passing is not permitted.
2. Passing on the right is permitted when the way ahead is clear.
3. Passing on the left is permitted when the way ahead is clear.

The correct answer is 3.

A broken yellow centerline next to your side of the road indicates that traffic may cross the centerline to pass from your side of the road.

the question 10. What usually causes a locked wheel skid?

1. Braking too hard at a slow speed
2. Braking lightly at a slow speed
3. Braking too hard at a fast speed

The correct answer is 3.

A locked wheel skid is most commonly caused by a driver braking too hard while traveling at a high speed. Drivers should use their brakes smoothly and gradually.

the question 11. If you become drowsy while driving, you should:

1. Try to fight it.
2. Take a break.
3. Take some caffeine pills.

The correct answer is 2.
If you start to feel tired while driving, drive to the first available rest stop or service area to take a break, nap, stretch, or change drivers. You should not rely on caffeine pills or energy drinks, as these are not a replacement for rest and may make your driving even more dangerous.

the question 12. When you are facing a green light and there are pedestrians in the intersection:

1. You must yield the right-of-way to pedestrians.
2. You have the right-of-way over pedestrians.
3. Pedestrians must wait for you to cross.

The correct answer is 1.
When facing a green light, you must yield to pedestrians and vehicles already in the intersection. Drivers must yield to pedestrians when turning on a steady green signal.

the question 13. When driving behind another vehicle at night, you should:

1. Keep your headlights on the low beam setting.
2. Use your high beam headlights until you are within 10 feet of the vehicle ahead.
3. Use your high beam headlights.

The correct answer is 1.

Use high beam headlights only when driving in rural areas and when other cars are not nearby. Lower your headlights to their low beam setting when you are following closely behind another driver.

the question 14. Which of these statements is true about large trucks?

1. They take longer to stop than passenger vehicles.
2. They all have air brakes that allow them to stop quickly.
3. They are more maneuverable than passenger vehicles.

The correct answer is 1.

Large trucks take longer to stop than other vehicles traveling at the same speed. The average passenger vehicle traveling at 55 mph can stop within 400 feet. However, a large truck traveling at the same speed can take almost 800 feet to stop.

the question 15. It is a very windy day. You are driving and a dust storm blows across the freeway, reducing your visibility. You should decrease your speed and turn on your:

1. Interior lights.
2. Parking lights.
3. Headlights.

The correct answer is 3.

Drivers must use their headlights any time conditions prevent them from seeing other vehicles. Conditions with lowered visibility include dust, clouds, rain, snow, smoke, or fog on or near the roadway.

the question 16. This sign means:

1. Traffic signal ahead.
2. Stop.
3.Yield the right-of-way.

The correct answer is 1.

This sign warns of an approaching traffic signal.

the question 17. You want to park downhill on a two-way road and there is no curb. Which way do you turn your front wheels?

1. Straight ahead
2. Right, toward the side of the road
3. Left, toward the center of the road

The correct answer is 2.

When parking facing downhill on a road with or without a curb, or when facing uphill on a road without a curb, turn your front wheels toward the edge of the road so your vehicle will roll away from traffic if the brakes fail. However, when parking uphill on a road with a curb, turn your wheels toward the center of the road so the vehicle will roll into the curb if the brakes fail.

the question 18. If you drive 55 mph in a 55 mph zone you can be given a speeding ticket:
1. Under no circumstances because it is always legal.
2. If the road or weather conditions require a slower speed.
3. Only if you are approaching a sharp curve in the road.

The correct answer is 2.

California has a "Basic Speed Law," which means that you may never drive faster than would be safe in current conditions. Even if your speed is slower than the posted limit, you may still be cited if you are going too fast for conditions. When deciding how quickly to drive, drivers should take multiple factors into account, such as the speed of surrounding vehicles, the condition of the road surface, the presence of bicyclists and pedestrians, and weather conditions.

the question 19. This symbol is used for:

1. Dangerous intersections.
2. Slow-moving vehicles.
3. Yield signs.

The correct answer is 2.

A reflective orange triangle on the rear of a vehicle means it travels only at slow speeds. You may see this sign on roadwork equipment, farm vehicles, or horse-drawn wagons and carriages. It appears as a solid orange triangle during the day and a hollow red triangle at night.

he question 20. You want to turn left at an upcoming corner. Yield the right-of-way to:

. Oncoming vehicles also turning left.
. All approaching vehicles.
. Pedestrians on the sidewalk waiting for a "Walk" ignal.

The correct answer is 2.

When making a left turn, you must yield to pedestrians, bicyclists, or other vehicles moving on their green light.

the question 21. When driving in fog, you should:

1. Use your high beam headlights.
2. Use your parking lights.
3. Use your low beam headlights.

The correct answer is 3.
Drivers should use low beam headlights when driving in fog.
High beams will reflect back at the driver, making it difficult
to see.

the question 22. California's Move Over law requires:

1. All vehicles to stay in the right lane at all times.
2. Trucks to use the left lane.
3. All vehicles to vacate the lane closest to an
emergency vehicle that is stopped with its lights
flashing.

The correct answer is 3.

If an emergency vehicle with its lights on is stopped on the
side of the road, California drivers are required to vacate the
lane directly next to the vehicle, if possible. If a driver cannot
move over safely, they must slow down and proceed with
caution. This law also applies when approaching a stopped
tow truck or Department of Transportation vehicle.

the question 23. When you drive through a construction zone, you should:

1. Stop to watch the workers.
2. Decrease your following distance.
3. Pass the construction zone carefully and not "rubberneck."

The correct answer is 3.

To avoid contributing to chronic traffic congestion, you should not "rubberneck." That is, you should not slow down to look at out-of-the-ordinary things.

the question 24. To help avoid skidding on slippery surfaces, you should:

1. Shift to a lower gear after starting down a steep hill.
2. Speed up to enter curves and slow down to exit them.
3. Slow down before entering curves and intersections.

The correct answer is 3.

Slow down before you enter a curve because you do not know what may be ahead. Braking on a curve may cause you to skid.

the question 25. Which of the following is true about vehicles displaying a diamond-shaped sign that indicates a hazardous load?

1. They are not allowed to drive on freeways.
2. They must stop before crossing railroad tracks.
3. They are not allowed to exceed 35 mph.

The correct answer is 2.

Vehicles displaying hazardous load signs are required to stop before crossing railroad tracks.

the question 26. Drivers turning left must yield to:

1. Oncoming vehicles traveling straight or turning right
2. Passing cars.
3. No one in particular.

The correct answer is 1.

Drivers making a left turn must yield to all vehicles approaching from the opposite direction. This includes bicycles and motorcycles.

the question 27. This sign means:

1. No right turn.
2. You must turn right.
3. Watch for traffic on your right.

The correct answer is 1.

This sign prohibits right turns. You cannot make a right turn at an intersection where this sign is posted.

the question 28. When can you drive in a bike lane?

1.   During rush hour traffic if there are no bicyclists in the bike lane.
2. When you are within 200 feet of a cross street where you plan to turn right.
3. When you want to pass a driver ahead of you who is turning right.

The correct answer is 2.

If there is a bike lane, drive into the bike lane no more than 200 feet before a turn. Watch for bicyclists or motorcyclists who may get between your vehicle and the curb.

the question 29. When parking uphill on a two-way street with no curb, your front wheels should be:

1. Turned to the left (toward the street).
2. Turned to the right (away from the street).
3. Parallel with the pavement.

The correct answer is 2.

When parking on a hill (either uphill or downhill) where there is no curb, you should turn your wheels so that the vehicle will roll away from the center of the road if the brakes fail.

the question 30. You are required to stop your vehicle:

1. At any intersection where a police officer orders you to stop.
2. Where there is a red traffic light.
3. Both of the above.

The correct answer is 3.

You must come to a complete stop at a steady or flashing red traffic light. You must always obey instructions given by officers directing traffic, regardless of any posted signs or traffic signals.

the question 31. If a traffic signal light is not working, you must:

1. Stop, then proceed when safe.
2. Stop before entering the intersection and let all other traffic go first.
3. Slow down or stop, only if necessary.

The correct answer is 1.
If a traffic signal is not working and no lights are showing, you should proceed cautiously as if the intersection is controlled by stop signs in all directions.

the question 32. A vehicle suddenly cuts in front of you, creating a hazard. What should you do first?

Honk and step on the brake firmly.
Take your foot off the gas pedal.
Swerve into the lane next to you.

The correct answer is 2.
If a vehicle merges in front of you too closely, take your foot off of the accelerator. This will create space between you and the vehicle ahead without requiring you to slam on your brakes or swerve into another lane.

the question 33. If your vehicle has a mechanical problem:

1. Signal and pull into the slow lane.
2. Stop in your lane and put on your hazard lights.
3. Put on your hazard lights and pull off the road.

The correct answer is 3.

If your vehicle breaks down on a highway, make sure other drivers can see it. Get your vehicle off the road and away from traffic if at all possible and turn on your emergency flashers to show that you are having trouble.

the question 34. This sign means:

1. Two-way traffic.
2. Change in direction ahead.
3. School zone and crossing.

The correct answer is 1.

This sign informs drivers that they are leaving a divided roadway and approaching a two-way highway.

the question 35. You must show proof of insurance to law enforcement:

1. Only if you are involved in a collision.
2. If you are involved in a collision or stopped for a citation.
3. Only if you are stopped and cited.

The correct answer is 2.

You must have evidence of financial responsibility, such as proof of insurance, with you whenever you drive. You must always show proof of insurance and your license to an officer upon request after a traffic stop or collision.

the question 36. U-turns in business districts are:

Always illegal because they are dangerous.
Legal whenever oncoming vehicles are not a hazard.
Legal at intersections, unless a sign prohibits them.

The correct answer is 3.

In a business district, you may make a U-turn only at an intersection, unless a sign prohibits it, or where openings are provided for turns.

CALIFORNIA DMV Written TEST #7

the question 1. On freezing, wet days, which of the following roadways is most likely to hide spots of ice?

1. Roadways near the tops of hills
2. Roadways on bridges and overpasses
3. Roadways paved with asphalt

The correct answer is 2.

Bridges and overpasses tend to freeze before the rest of the road does. They can hide spots of ice.

the question 2. Hydroplaning occurs when tires ride on a thin film of water instead of on the surface of the road. To prevent hydroplaning in rainy weather, you should:

1. Put on your cruise control to maintain a constant speed.
2. Decrease your speed.
3. Move to the shoulder of the road as soon as it starts to rain.

The correct answer is 2.

In rainy weather, you should lower your speed to reduce the risk of hydroplaning. Driving too fast may cause your tires to ride up on the water and lose contact with the surface of the road, making it very difficult to control your vehicle.

the question 3. This yellow warning sign means:

1. You are approaching a school or school crosswalk.
2. Slow down, drive with caution, and watch for children.
3. Both of the above.

The correct answer is 3.

This sign is placed on roads near schools to warn drivers to slow down, drive with caution, and watch for children.

the question 4. A flashing red traffic light at an intersection means:

1. Slow down before entering.
2. Stop before entering.
3. Stop and wait for the green light.

The correct answer is 2.

A flashing red signal means "stop." After coming to a stop, you may proceed once it is safe, observing all right-of-way rules.

the question 5. Fines in a construction zone are:

1. Doubled.
2. Tripled.
3. Cut in half.

The correct answer is 1.
Fines for moving traffic violations are doubled in highway construction or maintenance zones where workers are present. When operating in a construction zone, you must drive carefully and follow all directions provided by signs, signals, officers, and flaggers.

he question 6. In inclement weather, you should:

1. Steer off the road.
2. Drive in a low gear.
3. Steer and brake smoothly.

The correct answer is 3.
When driving during unfavorable weather conditions, avoid jamming on the brakes and making sharp, quick turns. These behaviors will make controlling your vehicle in inclement weather even more difficult.

the question 7. There is no crosswalk and you see a pedestrian crossing your lane ahead. You should:

1. Make eye contact with and then pass the pedestrian
2. Slow down as you pass the pedestrian.
3. Stop and let the pedestrian finish crossing the street

The correct answer is 3.

At an intersection where traffic is not controlled by traffic signal lights, drivers are required to yield the right-of-way to pedestrians within any crosswalk, marked or unmarked. Even if there is no crosswalk, yield to the pedestrian.

the question 8. This sign means:

1. No passing zone.
2. Slow-moving vehicle.
3. Two-way traffic.

The correct answer is 1.

A triangular yellow sign with black lettering indicates a no passing zone. It will appear on the left side of a two-way, two lane roadway at the beginning of an area where prohibitive pavement markings are also used.

the question 9. When approaching a roundabout, you should always:

1. Increase your speed.
2. Decrease your speed.
3. Maintain your speed.

The correct answer is 2.
When approaching a roundabout, slow down. A roundabout is designed to be driven at a low speed.

the question 10. This yellow sign means:

1. There is a sharp turn to the right.
2. The lane must turn right.
3. A right turn is permitted on a green arrow only.

The correct answer is 1.
Some warning signs have a fluorescent yellow-green background. These signs warn of upcoming conditions, including roads with curves and sharp turns.

the question 11. When taking any medicine, you should:

Consult your doctor about the effects before driving.
Have someone follow you home.
Keep your window open and drive more slowly.

the question 12. To improve visibility lowered by rain or fog, drivers should use their:

1. Low beam headlights.
2. High beam headlights.
3. Parking lights.

the question 13. The speed limit at an uncontrolled railroad crossing is:

1. 25 mph.
2. 15 mph.
3. 20 mph.

The correct answer is 2.

When you are within 100 feet of an uncontrolled railroad crossing where you cannot see the tracks for 400 feet in both directions, the speed limit is 15 mph.

the question 14. A broken yellow line beside a solid yellow line indicates that passing is:

1. Permitted from the side next to the solid yellow line.
2. Not permitted from either direction.
3. Permitted from the side next to the broken yellow line.

The correct answer is 3.

When the center of the road is marked by a solid yellow line beside a broken yellow line, passing is permitted from the side next to the broken line and prohibited from the side next to the solid line.

the question 15. This sign means:

1. No U-turn.
2. No left turn.
3. No right turn.

NO RIGHT TURN

the question 16. You may drive off of the paved roadway to pass another vehicle:

1. If the shoulder is wide enough to accommodate
2. your vehicle.
2. If the vehicle ahead of you is turning left.
3. Under no circumstances.

the question 17. To turn left from a one-way street with multiple lanes onto a two-way street, start the turn in:

1. The far left lane.
2. Any available lane.
3. The lane closest to the middle of the street.

The correct answer is 1.
When making a left turn from a one-way street onto a two-way street, start from the far left lane.

the question 18. You want to make a right turn at the corner. A pedestrian with a guide dog is at the corner ready to cross the street in front of you. Before making your right turn, you should:

1. Turn off your engine until the person crosses the street.
2. Tell the pedestrian when to cross the street.
3. Wait until the person crosses the street.

The correct answer is 3.
Pedestrians using guide dogs or white canes (with or without a red tip) must be given the right-of-way at all times.

the question 19. If you are getting tired while driving, you should:

1. Stop and either get rest or change drivers.
2. Drink something with caffeine.
3. Open a window.

The correct answer is 1.

To avoid the dangers of fatigued driving, take breaks every hour or so during a long trip. If possible, share driving responsibilities with another person so you can each sleep while the other person drives.

the question 20. California's "Basic Speed Law" says:

1. You should never drive faster than posted speed limits.
2. You should never drive faster than is safe for current conditions.
3. The maximum speed limit in California is 70 mph o certain freeways.

The correct answer is 2.

The "Basic Speed Law" means that you may never drive faster than would be safe in current conditions. For example, if you drive 45 mph in a 55 mph zone during a dense fog, even though you are below the posted limit, you may be cited for driving too fast for conditions.

the question 21. If you pass a school bus that is stopped with its red lights flashing, you will:

1. Be fined up to $1,000.
2. Be fined up to $100.
3. Face no legal consequences.

The correct answer is 1.

Drivers must come to a complete stop when approaching a school bus stopped with its red lights flashing. Failure to stop until the red lights stop flashing may result in license suspension and a fine of up to $1,000.

the question 22. This yellow sign means:

1. One lane ahead.
2. Merging traffic ahead.
3. Lane ends ahead.

The correct answer is 2.

This sign warns of the possible presence of merging traffic.

the question 23. You want to pass a bicyclist in a narrow traffic lane when an oncoming vehicle is approaching. You should:

1. Honk your horn then pass the bicyclist.
2. Slow down and let the vehicle pass you before you pass the bicyclist.
3. Wait until the bicyclist rides off the roadway.

The correct answer is 2.

In this situation, you should take on one danger at a time. Rather than trying to squeeze between the bicyclist and the other vehicle, you should slow down to let the other vehicle pass, and then pass the bicyclist when it is safe to do so.

the question 24. You are driving behind a motorcycle and want to pass. You must:

1. Stay in the right lane as much as possible because the motorcycle is small and doesn't use all of the lane.
2. Blow your horn to make the motorcycle move onto the shoulder so that you can pass.
3. Have your vehicle entirely in the left lane before and during the pass.

The correct answer is 3.

When passing a motorcycle, allow a full lane to the motorcycle. Never crowd into the same lane as the motorcycle. Returning to the original lane too soon can force a rider to swerve to the right and into traffic or off the road.

the question 25. To avoid hydroplaning while driving in rainy conditions, you should:

1. Drive at a speed appropriate for ideal conditions.
2. Apply your brakes as soon as your car starts to skid.
3. Slow down.

The correct answer is 3.

When driving too quickly in wet conditions, your tires may lose all contact with the road surface. Loss of traction will cause the vehicle to ride on top of the water, which is called "hydroplaning." The best way to prevent this from happening is to drive more slowly in rainy or wet conditions than you would when driving during ideal weather conditions.

the question 26. It is legal to make a left turn at a red traffic light after stopping only if:

1. You are traveling on a two-way street and turning onto a two-way street.
2. You are traveling on a one-way street and turning onto another one-way street.
3. You yield to all other traffic at the intersection.

The correct answer is 2.

After coming to a complete stop, you may turn left at a red light only if you are traveling on a one-way street and turning onto another one-way street. Only make the turn if there are no posted signs prohibiting such a turn.

the question 27. This sign means:

1. Curves ahead.
2. Divided highway starts.
3. Divided highway ends.

The correct answer is 3.

Warning signs are usually yellow with black markings. This sign warns that the divided highway ends ahead. Prepare to change lanes or shift lane position.

the question 28. Which of the following increases your chances of being in a collision?

1. Looking over your shoulder while making lane changes
2. Continuously changing lanes to pass other vehicles
3. Adjusting your rearview mirror before you start driving

The correct answer is 2.

Every time you pass another vehicle, you increase your chance of being in a collision.

the question 29. If you come across livestock or other animals on the roadway, you should:

1. Swerve out of the way.
2. Slow down and stop.
3. Ignore them.

The correct answer is 2.

If you are driving and come across an animal of any kind in the road, try to slow down and stop if it's safe to do so. Swerving to avoid an animal can be dangerous because your vehicle may lose control and cause an accident.

the question 30. You have allowed the wheels of your vehicle to run off the edge of the pavement. What should you do first?

1. Turn the front wheels slightly to the left to edge the car back onto the pavement.
2. Hold the steering wheel firmly, release the gas pedal, and gently apply the brakes.
3. Apply the brakes and turn the front wheels sharply to the left.

The correct answer is 2.

If your vehicle leaves the roadway, hold the steering wheel firmly, release the gas pedal, and gently apply the brakes. Wait until your speed has reduced, check the traffic, and look for a place to safely return to the roadway by merging back into traffic. Overcompensating by jerking the wheel to return to the roadway can cause you to lose control of your vehicle or may cause your car to go into other lanes of traffic.

the question 31. While all of the following actions are dangerous to do while driving, which is also illegal?

1. Listening to music through a set of dual headphone
2. Adjusting your outside mirrors.
3. Reading a road map.

The correct answer is 1.

Listening to music through a set of dual headphones is dangerous and illegal.

the question 32. If there is a deep puddle on the road ahead, you should:

1. Maintain the posted speed to make it through the water.
2. Avoid the puddle if possible.
3. Shift into neutral as you drive through the water.

The correct answer is 2.

To prevent skidding on slippery surfaces, avoid especially slippery areas, such as ice patches, wet leaves, oil, or deep puddles. The safest surface for driving is a dry, solid surface.

the question 33. When making a right turn from a highway with two lanes traveling in your direction, you may turn from:

1. The lane closest to the center of the road.
2. The lane nearest the curb or edge of the roadway.
3. Either lane, depending on oncoming traffic.

The correct answer is 2.
Begin and end the turn in the lane nearest
the right-hand curb. Do not swing wide into another
lane of traffic.

the question 34. It is unlawful to:

1. Pass another vehicle in any marked no passing zone.
2. Pass another vehicle over a railroad crossing.
3. Both of the above.

The correct answer is 3.
It is illegal to cross the centerline to pass when driving on hills, in curves, and in other locations where you cannot see ahead far enough to pass safely. You may not pass at street crossings, at railroad crossings, where signs indicate no passing zones, or where a solid yellow line is next to your lane. You may not pass when the vehicle in front of you has stopped for a pedestrian or when driving in work zones where passing would be hazardous.

the question 35. Which of the following are factors commonly contributing to traffic crashes?

1. Exceeding the posted speed limit and driving too fast for conditions or circumstances.
2. Getting adequate rest and staying alert.
3. Scanning the environment and staying focused on the driving task.

The correct answer is 1.

Driving above the speed limit, driving too far below the speed limit, and driving too fast for conditions are all actions that commonly contribute to traffic accidents. Always drive with the general flow of traffic, within legal speed limits.

the question 36. This red and white sign means you should:

1. Stop and check for traffic coming from both directions before proceeding.
2. Give the right-of-way to traffic on the road you wish to enter or cross.
3. Maintain a steady speed and check for traffic coming from all directions.

The correct answer is 2.

A three-sided yield sign indicates that you must slow down and be ready to stop, if necessary, to let any vehicle, bicyclist, or pedestrian pass before you proceed. In this case, you do not have the right-of-way.

CALIFORNIA DMV Written TEST #8

the question 1. When driving at night, you should:

1. Always use your high beams.
2. Look directly at the headlights of an oncoming vehicle.
3. Increase your following distance.

The correct answer is 3.

Increase your following distance when it is difficult to see due to darkness. Use headlights to increase visibility, following the rules for proper use of high beams and low beams. Avoid looking directly at the headlights of an oncoming vehicle to avoid being blinded by the glare.

the question 2. This road sign means:

1. School crossing.
2. Pedestrian crossing.
3. Jogging trail.

The correct answer is 2.

Warning signs are usually yellow with black markings.

This sign indicates the presence of a crosswalk, regardless of if it is marked on the pavement or not. Upon seeing this sign, you should be alert and allow any pedestrians to cross the road safely.

the question 3. Your driving lane is next to a bicycle lane. You want to make a right turn at the upcoming intersection. You:

1. May not enter the bicycle lane to make your turn.
2. Should only merge into the bicycle lane if you stop before turning.
3. Must merge into the bicycle lane before making your turn.

The correct answer is 3.
When you are making a right turn, you must enter the bicycle lane no more than 200 feet before the corner or driveway entrance. Do not drive a motor vehicle in the bicycle lane at any other time.

he question 4. Which of the following substances can affect the ability to drive?

1. Tranquilizers, marijuana, and sedatives.
2. Cough syrups and cold tablets containing codeine or antihistamines.
3. All of the above.

The correct answer is 3.
A number of drugs can impair your ability to drive, including depressant medications like tranquilizers and sedatives; over-the-counter cough syrups, cold tablets, and allergy medications (which may contain impairing substances like alcohol, codeine, or antihistamines); and illegal drugs.

the question 5. This sign is a warning that you are approaching:

1. An intersection.
2. A crosswalk.
3. A railroad crossing.

The correct answer is 3.

A round sign means you are approaching a railroad crossing. This sign is posted a few hundred feet in front of the tracks and tells drivers to slow down, look, listen, and prepare to stop.

the question 6. This white sign means you:

1. May turn left only on a green arrow.
2. May turn left on a green light when it is safe.
3. Must wait for the solid green light before you turn left.

The correct answer is 2.

A sign that says to "yield" means that you must slow down and be ready to stop to let any vehicle, bicyclist, or pedestrian pass before you proceed. After yielding, you may follow the remaining directions on the sign.

the question 7. Backing your vehicle is:

1. Always dangerous.
2. Dangerous if you have a helper.
3. Only dangerous in large vehicles.

The correct answer is 1.

Backing up is always dangerous because it is hard to see behind your vehicle. Use extra caution when backing up.

the question 8. An orange-colored sign like this means:

1. There is roadwork ahead.
2. You must change lanes ahead.
3. There is a detour ahead.

The correct answer is 1.

Orange-colored signs indicate construction areas. Proceed with caution.

the question 9. When driving in fog, it is best to drive with:

1. High beam headlights.
2. Low beam headlights.
3. Four-way flashers.

The correct answer is 2.

Use low beam headlights when driving in fog, rain, or snow. High beams may reflect off of the weather and make visibility even poorer.

the question 10. Only _____ can lower blood alcohol concentration (BAC) and reduce alcohol's effects on a body.

1. Drinking caffeine
2. Eating foods high in fat
3. Time

The correct answer is 3.

The only way to sober up after drinking alcohol is to allow time for your body to eliminate the alcohol in your system. Nothing you can do, including eating and drinking, can accelerate this process.

the question 11. A police officer is signaling for you to continue driving through a red light. What should you do?

1. Do as the officer tells you.
2. Wait for the green light.
3. Stop first, then do what the officer tells you.

The correct answer is 1.

You must obey any traffic direction, order, or signal given by a traffic officer, peace officer, or firefighter, even if it conflicts with existing signs, signals, or laws.

the question 12. When you see this sign, you should stop and:

1. Check for vehicles only in the direction that you plan on going, then proceed.
2. Let all vehicles that arrive before or after you go first.
3. Check for traffic in all directions before proceeding.

The correct answer is 3.

At a stop sign, you must come to a full stop and check for traffic in all directions before proceeding.

the question 13. You are preparing to exit the interstate. When should you start reducing your speed?

1. About halfway through the deceleration lane.
2. As you approach the deceleration lane.
3. Immediately upon entering the deceleration lane.

The correct answer is 3.

When leaving an interstate, you should maintain your speed until you enter the deceleration lane, at which point you should reduce your speed to the exit ramp's posted advisory speed.

the question 14. It is illegal to leave a child age six or younger unattended in a vehicle on a hot day:

1. Even if they are secured in a child passenger restraint system.
2. If they are supervised by a person twelve years of age or older.
3. Only if the key is in the ignition.

The correct answer is 1.

It is never a good idea to leave a child unattended in a car. It is illegal to leave a child age six or younger unattended in a vehicle. A child may be left under the supervision of a person age 12 or older.

the question 15. Blue traffic signs offer information on:

1. Motorist services.
2. Construction and maintenance.
3. Mileage information, such as distances to specific locations.

The correct answer is 1.

Blue signs on the roadway are service signs. They are used to provide information about motorist services, such as upcoming rest areas, food options, or nearby hospitals.

the question 16. At an intersection with stop signs on all corners, yield the right-of-way to any driver:

1. On your left.
2. Who arrived before you.
3. Across from your vehicle.

The correct answer is 2.

After coming to a full stop, vehicles should proceed through four-way stop in the order in which they arrive to the intersection. If multiple vehicles arrive at the same time, the vehicle on the left must yield the right-of-way to the vehicle on the right.

the question 17. All of the following are dangerous to do while driving. Which is also illegal?

1. Wearing a headset that covers both ears.
2. Having one or more interior lights on.
3. Using cruise control on residential streets.

The correct answer is 1.

It is illegal to drive while wearing a headset or earplugs in both ears.

the question 18. On a green arrow, you must:

1.   Yield to any vehicle, bicycle, or pedestrian in the intersection.
2. Yield to pedestrians only in the intersection.
3. Wait four seconds before proceeding.

The correct answer is 1.

A green arrow means "go." You must turn in the direction the arrow is pointing after you yield to any vehicles, bicycles, or pedestrians who are still in the intersection.

the question 19. You consent to take a chemical test for the alcohol content of your blood, breath, or urine:

1. Only if you have been drinking alcohol.
2. Whenever you drive in California.
3. Only if you have a collision.

The correct answer is 2.

By driving in California, you consent to have your breath, blood, or urine tested if you are arrested for suspicion of driving under the influence of alcohol and/or drugs.

the question 20. You must look for bicyclists in the same lanes used by motor vehicles because they:

1. Must ride facing oncoming traffic.
2. Illegally share lanes with motor vehicles.
3. Are entitled to share the road with motor vehicles.

The correct answer is 3.

Bicyclists have the right to operate on the road and may lawfully be permitted to ride on certain sections of freeways where there is no alternate route and bicycling is not forbidden by a sign. Watch for bicyclists and share the road when they are present.

the question 21. A steady green traffic light at an intersection means:

1. Increase your speed.
2. Adjust your mirrors.
3. You may continue through the intersection at a safe and reasonable speed, if it is clear to do so.

The correct answer is 3.

A steady green traffic light indicates that the driver may continue through the intersection. The driver should yield to traffic or pedestrians already in the intersection and proceed when the intersection is clear.

the question 22. Slowing down just to look at collisions or anything else out-of-the-ordinary:

1. Causes traffic congestion.
2. Prevents rear-end collisions.
3. Improves traffic flow by preventing collisions.

The correct answer is 1.

Avoid "rubbernecking," or slowing down to look at collisions or anything else out-of-the-ordinary. This helps to relieve traffic congestion.

the question 23. When should drivers yield the right-of-way to pedestrians in a crosswalk?

1. Only if the pedestrians first wave to the driver.
2. Only if the pedestrians are not texting while walking.
3. At all times.

The correct answer is 3.

Bring your vehicle to a complete stop at a crosswalk to yield the right-of-way to any vehicle or pedestrian already in the intersection. You may carefully proceed if your lane is completely clear.

the question 24. It is illegal for a person 21 years of age or older to drive with a blood alcohol concentration (BAC) that is _____ or higher.

1. 0.08% -- Eight-hundredths of one percent
2. 0.10% -- One-tenth of one percent
3. 0.05% -- Five-hundredths of one percent

The correct answer is 1.

For drivers age 21 or older, it is illegal to drive with a blood alcohol concentration (BAC) of 0.08 percent or higher. Driving while under the influence of alcohol is not only illegal, but dangerous.

the question 25. Which way do you turn your front wheels to park downhill next to a curb?

1. Into the curb
2. Away from the curb
3. Parallel to the curb

The correct answer is 1.

When parking downhill, turn your front wheels into the curb or toward the side of the road. Set the parking brake.

the question 26. What does this road sign mean?

1. Be ready to merge with traffic entering your lane.
2. Always stop.
3. Divided highway ahead.

The correct answer is 1.

Warning signs are usually yellow with black markings.

This sign warns that merging traffic will be entering from the right, so drivers should prepare to allow the incoming traffic to safely merge.

the question 27. As your speed increases, it is important to:

1. Turn on your headlights.
2. Look well ahead of your vehicle.
3. Change lanes frequently.

The correct answer is 2.
Your vehicle's stopping distance increases as your speed increases. When driving at high speeds, it is important to look well ahead of your vehicle to allow yourself space to safely react to hazardous situations.

the question 28. A curb painted blue means parking is:

1. Allowed for no longer than 15 minutes.
2. Only allowed when picking up or dropping off passengers.
3. For disabled persons with a special placard or plate.

The correct answer is 3.
A blue curb indicates an area where parking is permitted only for a disabled person, or driver of a disabled person, who displays a placard or special license plate for disabled persons or disabled veterans.

the question 29. Prior to entering a curve:

1. Activate your turn signal.
2. Reduce your speed.
3. Brake hard.

The correct answer is 2.

You may drive more slowly than the posted speed limit, based on road conditions, but it is illegal to drive any faster than the posted speed limit. Some conditions which require reduced speed for safety include approaching curves or hills where visibility is limited, driving on slippery roads, and driving on roads where animals and pedestrians are present.

the question 30. A red arrow pointing to the right on a traffic light means you may:

1. Turn in that direction after slowing and checking for traffic.
2. Not turn in that direction until the light turns green
3. Turn in that direction after you come to a complete stop.

The correct answer is 2.

A red arrow means "stop." You must remain stopped until a green light or green arrow appears. Do not turn against a red arrow.

the question 31. When driving in fog, you should use your:
1. Fog lights only.
2. High beams.
3. Low beams.

The correct answer is 3.
It is best to postpone driving until a fog clears. However, if you must drive in the fog, you should do so slowly and use your windshield wipers and low beam headlights.

the question 32. When changing lanes, you can check your blind spot by:

1. Using the inside rearview mirror.
2. Turning your head and looking over your shoulder.
3. Using your side mirror.

The correct answer is 2.
Even if your vehicle is properly equipped with mirrors, there are blind spots that cannot be seen by using the mirrors. Before changing lanes, look over your shoulder to check these areas.

the question 33. When you see this black and yellow sign, it means:

1. The road to the right is for one-way traffic only.
2. There is a detour to the right due to road construction.
3. The road ahead changes direction at an extreme angle.

The correct answer is 3.
Warning signs are usually yellow with black markings.
They alert you to conditions that are immediately ahead.
This sign tells drivers to slow down and prepare for an abrupt change in direction at an extreme angle.

the question 34. Having a driver license is a:

1. Requirement.
2. Privilege.
3. Right.

The correct answer is 2.
It is important to remember that driving is a privilege and that all drivers play a role in ensuring that everyone remains safe on the roadways. If you prove to be abusive of that privilege, the privilege may be revoked.

the question 35. What does this road sign mean?

1. Winding road
2. Loose gravel
3. Slippery when wet

The correct answer is 3.

This sign indicates that the road may be slippery when wet.
Exercise caution when driving on a slippery road.

the question 36. This white sign means you should not pass other vehicles:

1. Until after you pass the sign.
2. Unless it seems safe to do so.
3. For any reason.

The correct answer is 3.

A white rectangular sign indicates that you must obey
the stated rule. This sign means that drivers should not pass
other vehicles for any reason.

CALIFORNIA DMV Written TEST #9

The question 1. When passing another vehicle:

1. Pass the vehicle as slowly as possible.
2. Drive at the same speed as the vehicle you are passing.
3. Pass the vehicle as safely and as quickly as possible.

The correct answer is 3.
When passing another vehicle that is traveling in the same direction as you, pass quickly to resume visibility. Return to your previous lane only when you can see both of the vehicle's headlights in your rearview mirror.

The question 2. This sign indicates that:

1. There is a steep hill ahead.
2. No trucks are allowed on the upcoming hill.
3. A logging road is ahead.

The correct answer is 1.
Warning signs are usually yellow with black markings. This sign warns drivers about an upcoming steep hill. Drivers should slow down and be ready to control their speed and protect their brakes from damage.

the question 3. You should drive on the shoulder to pass a car:

1. If the vehicle ahead of you is turning left.
2. Under no circumstances.
3. If the shoulder is wide enough.

The correct answer is 2.

Passing on the right is permissible only if it is possible to do so without driving off the roadway. Never pass another vehicle on the shoulder because the other driver will not expect you to be there and may pull off the road.

the question 4. This sign means:

1. Merge right.
2. Divided highway begins.
3. Lane ends.

The correct answer is 3.

This sign indicates that the right lane ends ahead.

A merging maneuver will be required for drivers in that lane.

the question 5. To make a right turn at a corner, you:

1. May not enter the bicycle lane.
2. Should only merge into the bicycle lane if you stop before turning.
3. Must merge into the bicycle lane before turning.

The correct answer is 3.

When making a right turn where there is a bicycle lane, you must merge into the bicycle lane no more than 200 feet before the corner and then make the turn. Be sure there are no bicyclists in your path before merging.

the question 6. Which of the following statements about blind spots is true?
1.   Blind spots are eliminated if you have one outside mirror.
2. Large trucks have bigger blind spots than most passenger vehicles.
3. Blind spots can be checked by looking in your rearview mirror.

The correct answer is 2.

Even if a vehicle is properly equipped with rearview and outside mirrors, it still has blind spots that cannot be seen n the mirrors. Large trucks have much larger blind spots han most passenger vehicles.

the question 7. To know where traffic is behind you:

1. Frequently check your rearview mirror.
2. Turn and look out your back window.
3. Keep other vehicles out of your blind spots.

The correct answer is 1.

Drivers should check their rearview mirrors often to stay aware of the position of traffic behind them.

the question 8. Changing from one lane to another is best done:

1. Quickly and often.
2. When a car is in your blind spot.
3. Gradually and carefully.

The correct answer is 3.

You should always change lanes gradually and carefully. Only change lanes when necessary. Every lane change increases the possibility of a traffic accident.

the question 9. When parking your vehicle parallel to the curb on a level street:

1. Your front wheels must be turned toward the street.
2. Your wheels must be within 18 inches of the curb.
3. One of your rear wheels must touch the curb.

The correct answer is 2.

When parking alongside the curb on a level street, the front and back wheels of your vehicle must be parallel with and within 18 inches of the curb.

the question 10. This road sign means:

1. Watch for people crossing your path.
2. No passing zone.
3. Work zone ahead.

The correct answer is 3.

This orange warning sign tells drivers that an area of roadwork is upcoming. When traveling through a work zone, stay alert for temporary traffic control devices.

the question 11. When turning left at an intersection:

1. You should always yield to oncoming traffic and pedestrians.
2. Oncoming traffic and pedestrians should yield to you
3. You should never yield to oncoming traffic and pedestrians.

The correct answer is 1.

Drivers making left turns must yield to oncoming traffic that is traveling straight. Drivers must always yield to pedestrians.

the question 12. A solid yellow line next to a broken yellow line means that vehicles:

1. Driving in both directions may pass.
2. Next to the broken line may pass.
3. Next to the solid line may pass.

The correct answer is 2.

Yellow lines separate lanes of traffic moving in opposite directions. A broken yellow line next to your driving lane means that you may pass.

the question 13. You should not make sudden stops in front of large trucks and buses because:

1. Small vehicle drivers cannot adequately see large trucks and buses in their rearview mirrors.
2. Large trucks and buses, due to their size and weight, require longer distances to stop than smaller passenger vehicles.
3. Large trucks and buses travel at a higher speeds than small vehicles.

The correct answer is 2.

Large vehicles require longer distances to stop and accelerate than smaller vehicles do. Making a sudden stop in front of a large vehicle is dangerous because the other driver may not be able to stop in time to avoid a collision.

the question 14. This sign means:

. No U-turn.
. No turning.
. No left turn.

The correct answer is 1.

This sign indicates that you may not make a U-turn. You cannot turn around to go in the opposite direction an intersection where this sign is posted.

the question 15. To prevent tailgating, drivers should follow the:

1. One-second rule.
2. Two-second rule.
3. Three-second rule.

the question 16. You must yield the right-of-way to an emergency vehicle that is using its siren and flashing lights by:

1. Driving as closely to the right edge of the road as possible and stopping.
2. Moving into the right lane and driving slowly until has passed.
3. Stopping immediately, even if you are within an intersection.

the question 17. This is the shape and color of a ____
sign.

1. Stop
2. Wrong way
3. Yield

The correct answer is 3.
Downward-facing triangular signs mean drivers must yield.
When approaching a yield sign, slow down to a speed that is
reasonable for existing conditions and stop if necessary.
If you must stop, do so at a marked stop line, if it exists.

the question 18. When merging onto the freeway,
you should be driving:

1. At or near the speed of the freeway traffic.
2. At the legal speed limit.
3. More slowly than the freeway traffic.

The correct answer is 1.
You should enter a freeway at or near the speed of traffic,
unless the speed of traffic exceeds the legal speed limit.

the question 19. Check your rearview mirrors:

1. Often to see how traffic is moving behind you.
2. To see if a vehicle is in your blind spot.
3. Only when you are slowing down.

The correct answer is 1.

When driving, do not develop a fixed stare. Frequently check your rearview mirrors so you know the positions of vehicles near you.

the question 20. Which of the following is true about roadways on bridges and overpasses in cold, wet weather?

1. They tend to freeze before the rest of the road does
2. They do not freeze because they are made of concrete.
3. They tend to freeze after the rest of the road does.

The correct answer is 1.

Bridges and overpasses tend to freeze before the rest of the road does. They can hide spots of ice.

the question 21. You have been involved in a minor traffic collision with a parked vehicle and you can't find the owner. You must:

1. Leave a note on the vehicle.
2. Report the collision without delay to the city police or, in unincorporated areas, to the California Highway Patrol.
3. Both of the above.

The correct answer is 3.

If you collide with a parked car or other property, leave a note with your name, phone number, and address securely attached to what you hit. You must report the collision to the local city police or, if the collision was in an unincorporated area, to the California Highway Patrol (CHP).

the question 22. Use your headlights on rainy, snowy, or foggy days:
1. To keep your engine warm.
2. So others can see your vehicle.
3. To warn others of bad weather conditions.

The correct answer is 2.

On rainy, snowy, or foggy days, it may be difficult for other drivers to see your vehicle. Under these conditions, headlights make your vehicle easier to see. If the weather requires you to turn on your windshield wipers, you must also turn on your low beam headlights.

the question 23. When entering traffic after being parked at a curb, you:

1. Should drive more slowly than other traffic for 200 feet.
2. Should wait for a large enough gap to get up to the speed of traffic.
3. Should wait for the first two vehicles to pass, then drive into the lane.

The correct answer is 2.

Any time that you merge into city or highway traffic, you should wait for a gap in traffic large enough for your vehicle to get up to the speed of other traffic.

the question 24. If weather or light conditions require you to have your lights on while driving:

1. Use your parking lights.
2. Use your high beams.
3. Use your low beams.

The correct answer is 3.

Use your low beam headlights when driving in foggy, snowy, or rainy conditions. Light from high beam headlights will reflect back, causing glare and making it even more difficult to see ahead.

The question 25. There is a vehicle stopped on the right shoulder of the road with its hazard lights on. You should:

1. Change lanes to the left and speed up.
2. Slow down and pass very carefully.
3. Stop your vehicle until you can see what has happened.

The correct answer is 2.

If you see a vehicle's hazard lights ahead, slow down. There may be a collision or other road emergency ahead. Stop and give assistance if asked by anyone, or pass very carefully.

The question 26. If you drive faster than other vehicles on a road with one lane moving in each direction and continually pass the other cars, you will:

1. Get you to your destination much more quickly and safely.
2. Increase your chances of an collision.
3. Help prevent traffic congestion.

The correct answer is 2.

You should avoid passing other vehicles on two-lane roads. Every time you pass a vehicle, your odds of being in a collision increase.

the question 27. You should turn on your headlights:

1. One half hour after sunset.
2. When stopped at a railroad crossing.
3. When parked at a school.

The correct answer is 1.

Headlights must be used one half hour after sunset until one half hour before sunrise, when windshield wipers are being used due to rain or snow, and in any other situation when visibility is less than 1,000 feet. They should be used when a car is being driven on a small country or mountain road, even in sunny weather.

the question 28. This sign means:

1. Trucks entering.
2. Truck exit only.
3. Steep downgrade ahead.

The correct answer is 3.

This sign warns that a steep downgrade is ahead on the road. Drivers should check their brakes.

the question 29. You should signal continuously while turning because it:

1. Is illegal to turn off your signal before completing a turn.
2. Lets other drivers know what your intentions are.
3. Is always unsafe to turn off a signal before completing a turn.

The correct answer is 2.

You should always signal when turning, changing lanes, slowing down, or stopping so that other drivers, motorcyclists, bicyclists, and pedestrians will know your intentions.

the question 30. You are approaching an intersection with a steady yellow traffic light. If you have not already entered the intersection, you should:

1. Speed up to beat the red light.
2. Reduce you speed and proceed carefully through the intersection.
3. Come to a safe stop.

The correct answer is 3.

When a steady yellow light appears on a traffic signal, you should prepare to stop. If you are already within the intersection, you should clear the intersection as quickly as possible.

the question 31. If you are involved in a traffic collision, you are required to complete and submit a written report to the DMV:

1. Only if you or the other driver is injured.
2. If there is property damage in excess of $1,000 or if there are any injuries.
3. Only if you are at fault.

The correct answer is 2.

If a collision results in death, any minor or major injury, or more than $1,000 in damage to anyone's property, each driver involved must file a report with the DMV within 10 days. In some cases, the driver's insurance agent, broker, or legal representative may file the report to represent the driver.

the question 32. When you see this yellow sign, you should:

1. Always stop at the crosswalk.
2. Stop at the crosswalk until a crossing guards signals for you to go.
3. Be prepared to stop if children are in the crosswalk.

The correct answer is 3.

A five-sided sign indicates that you are near a school. Be aware and stop if children are in the crosswalk.

the question 33. You just sold your vehicle. You must notify the DMV within _____ days.

1. Five
2. 10
3. 15

The correct answer is 1.
When you sell or transfer a vehicle, you must notify the DMV within five days.

the question 34. If you are driving near a large commercial vehicle, you should:

1. Follow the large vehicle closely to reduce wind drag on your vehicle.
2. Avoid driving beside it for long stretches of time.
3. Drive on its right side when on curves and hills.

The correct answer is 2.
Because large commercial vehicles have large blind spots on each side, you should avoid driving beside them for long periods of time.

the question 35. Always stop before crossing railroad tracks when:

1. There isn't room on the other side for you to completely cross the tracks.
2. The railroad crossing is located in a city or town that has frequent train traffic.
3. You are transporting two or more young children in a passenger vehicle.

The correct answer is 1.

Expect a train on any track, at any time, traveling in either direction. If you need to stop after crossing the tracks, wait until you can completely cross the tracks before proceeding. Make sure your vehicle clears the tracks before you stop.

the question 36. Before returning to your original lane after passing another vehicle, you should:

1. Beep your horn.
2. See both headlights of the passed vehicle in your rearview mirror.
3. Flash your headlights.

The correct answer is 2.

When passing is permitted, look for both headlights of the passed vehicle in your rearview mirror. Only then may you safely return to your original lane.

CALIFORNIA DMV Written TEST #10

the question 1. If you approach a flashing red traffic light, you:

1. Are traveling in the wrong direction.
2. Must treat the intersection as if it is controlled by a stop sign.
3. May not proceed until it changes to green.

The correct answer is 2.

Treat a flashing red light the same as a stop sign. Come to a complete stop at the stop line or, if there is no stop line, prior to the crosswalk and before entering the intersection. Yield to all other traffic and pedestrians.

the question 2. When driving at night, you should:

1. Always use your high beams.
2. Look directly at the headlights of an oncoming vehicle.
3. Increase your following distance.

The correct answer is 3.

Driving at night is more hazardous than daytime driving because the lowered visibility makes it difficult to judge speed, distances, and other potential hazards. Increase your following distance to help prevent a potential collision if the vehicle in front of you should stop abruptly. Use your headlights when driving at night, following the rules for proper usage of high beams and low beams.

the question 3. This sign means:

1. Slippery when wet.
2. Stop sign ahead.
3. No U-turn.

The correct answer is 1.

All roads are slippery and dangerous when wet. This sign warns of conditions that can cause a driver to lose control of a car. A driver should slow down when coming upon wet pavement because it takes longer to stop.

the question 4. Placard abuse will result in:

1. Placard revocation only.
2. Only a fine.
3. Placard revocation, a fine, and/or jail time.

The correct answer is 3.

Abuse of a disabled placard or plate is a misdemeanor. Placard abuse can result in the loss of special parking privileges, a fine of up to $1,000, and up to six months of jail time.

the question 5. On rainy, snowy, or foggy days, turn on your windshield wipers and use your headlights:

1. On the high beam setting.
2. So other drivers can see you.
3. Only when driving on the freeway.

The correct answer is 2.

Turn on your headlights when it is cloudy, raining, snowing, or foggy. If weather conditions require you to use your windshield wipers, you are required to turn on your low beam headlights.

the question 6. You should use your horn when:

1. Another vehicle is in your way.
2. It may help prevent a collision.
3. Another driver makes a mistake.

The correct answer is 2.

Only use your horn when it is necessary to avoid collisions. Do not use your horn if a driver or bicyclist is moving slowly and you want him or her to drive faster or get out of your way.

the question 7. If you are feeling fatigued while driving, you should:

1. Increase your speed to reach your destination more quickly.
2. Increase the volume of your radio.
3. Find a safe parking area to take a short nap.

The correct answer is 3.

When driving, watch for warning signs of fatigue. You are too tired to drive safely if you are struggling to keep your eyes open, drifting from your lane, or turning up the radio and rolling down your windows to keep yourself awake. If you notice these signs, it is a good idea to find a safe place to park so you can refresh yourself with a short nap.

the question 8. You are driving on a one-way street. You may only turn left onto another one-way street if:

1. You increase your speed before the turn.
2. Traffic on the street moves to the right.
3. Traffic on the street moves to the left.

The correct answer is 3.

You may turn left onto a one-way street that moves to the left if there is no sign prohibiting the turn. You may not turn left onto a one-way street where traffic moves to the right.

the question 9. A diamond-shaped sign means:

1. Yield.
2. Stop.
3. Warning.

The correct answer is 3.

Diamond-shaped signs are used to warn drivers of special conditions or hazards ahead. They are typically yellow or orange in color.

the question 10. When may you legally drive around or under a railroad crossing gate?

1. Never.
2. When you can see clearly in both directions.
3. When the warning lights are not flashing.

The correct answer is 1.

Do not go around or under any lowered gate at a railroad crossing. Once the gate is raised, do not proceed across the tracks until you can see clearly in both directions and are sure there are no trains coming.

the question 11. A U-turn is not permitted:

1. In a parking lot.
2. On or near any curve or hill.
3. On a straight roadway with a clear view for 500 feet in both directions.

The correct answer is 2.
You must never turn around while on or near any curve or hill. You may not be able to see oncoming traffic or pedestrians and may cause a collision.

the question 12. Flash your brake lights or turn on your emergency flashers if you:

. Need to warn other drivers of a collision ahead.
. Are temporarily parked in a traffic lane to make delivery.
. Are backing out of a parking space.

The correct answer is 1.
If you can see a collision ahead, warn the drivers behind you by turning on your emergency flashers or by tapping your brake pedal quickly three or four times.

the question 13. At a railroad crossing, you must:

1. Watch for vehicles that must stop at all railroad crossings (school buses, trucks carrying hazardous materials, etc.).
2. Watch for multiple trains.
3. Both of the above.

The correct answer is 3.

You must approach all railroad crossings with extreme caution and cross only when you know that no train is coming from either direction. Be aware of vehicles that must stop at all railroad crossings, such as school buses and trucks carrying hazardous materials.

the question 14. If your vehicle has a two-part safety belt system, you should:

1. Use only the lap belt.
2. Use both the lap and shoulder belts.
3. Use only the shoulder belt.

The correct answer is 2.

If your vehicle has a two-part seat belt system, be sure to wear both the lap belt and the shoulder belt. Wearing either part alone greatly reduces your protection. If you have an automatic shoulder belt, be sure to buckle your lap belt as well.

the question 15. There are oncoming vehicles to your left and a row of parked vehicles to your right. You should steer:

1. Closer to the oncoming vehicles than the parked vehicles.
2. Closer to the parked vehicles than the oncoming vehicles.
3. A middle course between the oncoming and parked vehicles.

The correct answer is 3.

If there are oncoming vehicles to your left and a row of parked vehicles to your right, the best thing to do is to split the difference. Steer a middle course between the oncoming cars and the parked cars.

the question 16. Alcohol in any concentration is:

1. A stimulant.
2. A depressant.
3. Neither of the above.

The correct answer is 2.

Alcohol, in any concentration, is a depressant. It slows all nerve impulses and bodily functions, resulting in a lessening of inhibitions and negatively affecting a consumer's ability to concentrate and stay alert.

the question 17. At intersections, crosswalks, and railroad crossings, you should always:

1. Stop, listen, and proceed cautiously.
2. Look to the sides of your vehicle to see what is coming.
3. Slowly pass vehicles that seem to be stopped for no reason.

The correct answer is 2.

Any time you come to a place where people may cross or enter your path, or where one line of traffic meets another, you should look to the left and right sides of your vehicle to make sure no one is coming.

the question 18. This sign indicates a:

1. Railroad crossing.
2. Pedestrian crossing.
3. No passing zone.

The correct answer is 1.

Yellow signs with black markings are used to warn drivers about upcoming hazards or special conditions. Round signs are used only to warn about upcoming railroad crossings.

The question 19. You reach an intersection with stop signs on all four corners at the same time as the driver on your left. Who has the right-of-way?

1. The driver on your left has the right-of-way.
2. You have the right-of-way.
3. Whoever is signaling to make a turn has the right-of-way.

The correct answer is 2.
If two vehicles arrive at the same time to an intersection that has stop signs on all corners, the vehicle to the right has the right-of-way.

The question 20. You must stop at the intersection ahead. Just before the intersection, you have to cross railroad tracks. You should stop before crossing the railroad tracks when:

1. There isn't room on the other side for you to completely cross the tracks.
2. The crossing is located in a city or town with frequent train traffic.
3. You are transporting two or more children in a passenger vehicle.

The correct answer is 1.
If you need to stop after crossing railroad tracks, wait until you can completely cross the tracks before proceeding. Make sure your vehicle clears the tracks before you stop.

the question 21. You drive defensively when you:

1. Put one car length between you and the car ahead.
2. Look only at the car in front of you while driving.
3. Keep your eyes moving to look for possible hazards.

The correct answer is 3.

You are driving defensively when you are looking down the road for potential hazards. Constantly staring at the road directly in front of your vehicle is dangerous. As you scan ahead, be alert to vehicles around you.

the question 22. If pedestrians are illegally crossing in the middle of the street instead of in a crosswalk, you:

1. Must stop for them.
2. Do not have to stop for them.
3. Should honk your horn at them.

The correct answer is 1.

You must yield to pedestrians at all times. If the pedestrians are jaywalking or crossing the street where they should not be, you must still stop for them.

the question 23. You must file a report of a traffic accident occurring in California when:

1. Your vehicle fails a smog test.
2. You are involved in a collision and there is an injury.
3. You change your insurance company.

The correct answer is 2.
When you have a collision, report it to DMV within 10 days if anyone was injured (no matter how slightly) or killed. You or your representative must make this report whether or not you caused the collision, even if the collision occurred on private property.

the question 24. You may cross double yellow lines to pass another vehicle if the:

. Vehicle in front of you moves to the right to let you pass.
. Yellow line next to your side of the road is broken.
. Yellow line next to the opposite side of the road is broken.

The correct answer is 2.
A broken yellow line in the center of the road indicates that traffic next to the broken yellow line may pass, if it is safe to do so.

the question 25. A large truck is ahead of you and is turning right onto a street with two lanes in each direction. The truck:

1. May complete its turn in either of the two lanes.
2. May have to swing wide to complete the right turn.
3. Must stay in the right lane at all times while turning

The correct answer is 2.

When a vehicle makes a turn, the rear wheels follow a shorter path than the front wheels. The longer the vehicle, the bigger the difference between the paths of the front and rear wheels. Therefore, long trucks often have to swing wide to complete a right turn.

the question 26. When can you drive in a bike lane?

1. 30 minutes after sunset or 30 minutes before sunrise
2. On foggy days when visibility is low
3. 200 feet before making a turn

The correct answer is 3.

When you are making a right turn, you must enter the bicycle lane no more than 200 feet before the corner or driveway entrance. Do not drive in the bicycle lane at any other time

the question 27. You are crossing an intersection and an emergency vehicle is approaching while using its siren and flashing lights. You should:

1. Stop immediately in the intersection until it passes.
2. Pull to the right of the intersection and stop.
3. Continue through the intersection, pull to the right, and stop.

The correct answer is 3.

If you are in an intersection when you see an emergency vehicle approaching while using its flashing lights and/or siren, continue through the intersection and then drive to the right and stop. You must yield the right-of-way to any police vehicle, fire engine, ambulance, or other emergency vehicle using a siren or flashing lights.

the question 28. If a road is slippery, maintain a following distance that is:

1. No different than normal.
2. Farther from the car ahead than normal.
3. Closer to the car ahead than normal.

The correct answer is 2.

You need a longer distance to stop your vehicle on a slippery road than you do on a dry road. Maintain an increased following distance when driving on slippery roads.

the question 29. When driving on a slippery surface, such as snow or ice:

1. Shift to a low gear before going down steep hills.
2. Maintain traction by following other vehicles closely.
3. Pump your brakes to keep them from freezing.

The correct answer is 1.

To prevent skidding on slippery surfaces, you should shift to a low gear before going down a steep hill. You should also follow farther behind the vehicle in front of you than you normally would. Quick stops should be avoided. Unless you have antilock brakes, pump the brakes to slow or stop.

the question 30. Which of these vehicles must always stop before crossing railroad tracks?

1. Tank trucks with hazardous materials placards.
2. Motor homes or pickup trucks towing a boat trailer.
3. Sport utility vehicles carrying four or more persons.

The correct answer is 1.

A diamond-shaped sign on a truck means that the load on the truck is potentially dangerous (containing gas, explosives, etc. Vehicles displaying these signs are required to stop before crossing railroad tracks.

the question 31. What is the benefit of a space cushion around your vehicle?

1. Other drivers can cut in front of you, improving the flow of traffic.
2. If another driver makes a mistake, you have time to react.
3. It inflates to protect you from injury in the case of a collision.

The correct answer is 2.

Keeping space around your vehicle is important to ensure that you have time to safely react if another driver makes a mistake. For example, extra space around your vehicle may give you time to brake or maneuver out of the way of a vehicle veering into your lane.

the question 32. You can help keep the driver behind you a safe distance away from your vehicle by:

1. Driving 10 mph faster than the car behind you.
2. Driving 10 mph slower than the car behind you.
3. Maintaining a steady speed.

The correct answer is 3.

It is not always easy to maintain a safe distance behind your vehicle. However, you can help keep the driver behind you a safe distance away from your vehicle by maintaining a steady speed and signaling turns, lane changes, and deceleration in advance.

the question 33. If you have an argument with another person and you are angry, you should:

1. Loudly play the radio while driving so you won't think about your argument.
2. Take a few minutes to cool off before driving.
3. Drive on the interstate to let off steam.

The correct answer is 2.

Your emotions affect your ability to drive safely. If you are overly angry, excited, afraid, worried, or depressed, you should give yourself time to calm down before operating a vehicle. You need to be able to mentally focus on driving without thinking about the things that made you upset.

the question 34. Animals may be transported in the back of a pickup truck only if:

1. The sides of the truck bed are at least 18 inches high
2. They are properly secured.
3. The tailgate of the truck is closed.

The correct answer is 2.

An animal must not be transported in the back of a pickup or other truck unless the animal is properly secured to prevent it from falling, jumping, or being thrown from the vehicle.

the question 35. A peace officer is signaling for you to drive to the edge of the roadway. You decide to ignore the officer's warning and flee the scene. You are guilty of a misdemeanor and can be punished by being:

1. Fined up to $1,000.
2. Jailed in the county jail for not more than one year.
3. Given a warning and a citation.

The correct answer is 2.

Any person, while operating a motor vehicle, who willfully flees or attempts to evade a peace officer performing his or her duties is guilty of a misdemeanor punishable by imprisonment in a county jail for not more than one year.

the question 36. This road sign means:

1. You are about to enter a one-way street from the wrong direction.
2. U-turns are prohibited.
3. You may proceed if the way is clear.

The correct answer is 1.

This sign marks a one-way road, entrance, or exit. If you are facing this sign, traffic is coming toward you. Turn around if you are driving toward this sign.

CALIFORNIA DMV Written TEST #11

the question 1. This road sign means:

1. Bicycle crossing.
2. Stop only if other cars are approaching.
3. Yield the right-of-way to pedestrians.

The correct answer is 1.
Warning signs are usually yellow with black markings.
These signs alert drivers to areas where bicycles may
be crossing.

the question 2. You must obey instructions from
school crossing guards:

1. At all times.
2. Only during school hours.
3. Unless you do not see any children present.

The correct answer is 1.
Drivers should be alert to the presence of crossing guards
when near a school and must always obey their instructions.

the question 3. A broken yellow line beside a solid yellow line indicates that:

1. Passing is permitted from the lane next to the solid yellow line.
2. Passing is not permitted from either direction.
3. Passing is permitted from the lane next to the broken yellow line.

The correct answer is 3.

A broken yellow line alongside a solid yellow line means that traffic in the lane next to the broken line may cross the line to pass, while traffic in the lane next to the solid line may not.

the question 4. Roadways are the most slippery:

1. During a heavy downpour.
2. After it has been raining for awhile.
3. During the first rain after a dry spell.

The correct answer is 3.

Many roads are most slippery during the first rain after a dry spell because oil and dust on the road have not previously been washed away.

the question 5. You see a signal person at a road construction site ahead. You should obey his or her instructions:

1. Only if you see orange cones on the road ahead.
2. Unless they conflict with existing signs, signals, or laws.
3. At all times.

The correct answer is 3.

Obey special signs or instructions from flaggers. Driving carefully through work zones improves safety for drivers, pedestrians, bicyclists, and road workers.

the question 6. You were parked and have been waiting a long time with your turn signal on to re-enter traffic. However, traffic is heavy. You should:

1. Continue waiting and yielding to traffic in the lane.
2. Slowly inch your vehicle into the traffic lane.
3. Drive on the shoulder until a gap in traffic appears.

The correct answer is 1.

If you have been parked on the side of a road, you must yield to existing traffic when re-entering the road.

the question 7. All of the following practices are dangerous to do while driving. Which of these is also illegal?

1. Listening to music through headphones that cover both ears.
2. Adjusting your outside mirrors.
3. Transporting an unrestrained animal inside the vehicle.

The correct answer is 1.

Even people with good hearing cannot hear well if the radio or CD player is blaring. Do not wear a headset or earplugs in both ears while driving; it is against the law.

the question 8. If there is no crosswalk and you see a pedestrian crossing your lane, you should:

1. Make sure the pedestrian can see you before proceeding.
2. Cautiously drive around the pedestrian.
3. Stop and let the pedestrian finish crossing.

The correct answer is 3.

Drivers must always yield the right-of-way to pedestrians in the roadway, even if there is not a marked crosswalk.

The question 9. When preparing to make a left turn from a two-way street, you should drive:

1. Near the right-hand side of the road.
2. Near the centerline.
3. On the left of the centerline.

The correct answer is 2.
When you are turning left from a two-way street, begin in the lane closest to the centerline and start your turn just before the front of your car reaches the center of the intersection. Do not cut the corner. Steering hand-over-hand, turn into the first available legal lane.

The question 10. What is a potential effect of taking prescription drug while drinking alcohol?

1. There will likely be no effect.
2. It will make you more alert.
3. It can make you unfit to drive.

The correct answer is 3.
Legal medications, both prescription and over-the-counter, can impair your ability to drive. They can be particularly dangerous when used in combination with alcohol.

the question 11. While driving at night, a vehicle coming toward you has its high beams on, making it hard for you to see the road ahead. You should:

1. Look ahead toward the left edge of your lane.
2. Look ahead toward the right edge of your lane.
3. Look straight ahead in your lane.

The correct answer is 2.
If an oncoming driver fails to dim their high beams, you should avoid looking directly at the headlights. Instead, look toward the right edge of your lane and watch the oncoming vehicle out of the corner of your eye.

the question 12. You are approaching a railroad crossing with no warning devices and are unable to see 400 feet down the tracks in one direction. The speed limit is:

1. 15 mph.
2. 20 mph.
3. 25 mph.

The correct answer is 1.
Within 100 feet of a railroad crossing where you cannot see 400 feet down the tracks in both directions, the speed limit is 15 mph. However, you may drive faster if the crossing is controlled by gates, a warning signal, or a flagger.

the question 13. A white painted curb indicates a:

1. Loading zone for freight or passengers.
2. Loading zone for passengers or mail only.
3. Loading zone for freight only.

The correct answer is 2.
At a white painted curb, you may stop only long enough
to pick up or drop off passengers or mail.

the question 14. Highway pavement will be
particularly treacherous and most slippery:

1. If it has been raining several hours.
2. If it has just begun to rain.
3. If it has been raining for one to two hours.

The correct answer is 2.
Pavement is particularly treacherous when it first begins to
rain. Accumulations of dirt and oil mix with the rainwater,
creating a greasy film on the roadway.

the question 15. When you are merging onto the freeway, you should be driving:

1. At or near the speed of traffic on the freeway.
2. Five to 10 mph slower than the speed of traffic on the freeway.
3. The posted speed limit for freeway traffic.

The correct answer is 1.

When merging onto a freeway, you should enter at or near the speed of traffic.

the question 16. If you are about to be hit from the rear, you should consider each of the following, except for:

1. Applying your brakes.
2. Letting go of the steering wheel.
3. Pressing your head firmly against the head restraint

The correct answer is 2.

If your vehicle is hit from the rear while you are in forward motion, your body will be thrown backward. Press yourself against the back of your seat and put your head against the head restraint to prevent whiplash. Maintain a firm grip on the steering wheel and be ready to apply your brakes to avoid being pushed into another vehicle.

the question 17. It is against the law to enter an intersection when:

1. You can't get all the way across before the light turns red.
2. The light is flashing yellow and you didn't stop first.
3. The light is yellow and you cannot stop safely.

The correct answer is 1.

Do not enter an intersection if you cannot get completely across before the traffic signal light turns red. If you block the intersection, you can be cited.

the question 18. Drivers turning left must yield to:

1. Overtaking cars.
2. Oncoming cars.
3. No one.

The correct answer is 2.

Drivers turning left must yield to oncoming vehicles that are driving straight ahead. A turning driver may only proceed when they can safely turn without affecting oncoming traffic.

the question 19. If you want to pass a pedestrian who is walking along the roadway and an oncoming vehicle is approaching, you should:

1. Slow down and let the oncoming vehicle pass before you pass the pedestrian.
2. Keep driving at a steady speed. The oncoming vehicle must stop for you.
3. Honk your horn to get the pedestrian to move over.

The correct answer is 1.

If possible, try to only deal with one roadway hazard at a time. If you want to pass a pedestrian but an oncoming vehicle is approaching, slow down and let the vehicle pass. You may then pass the pedestrian if it is safe to do so.

the question 20. This sign means:

1. Trucks under 18,000 pounds are allowed.
2. Hill ahead.
3. Truck stop ahead.

The correct answer is 2.

Warning signs are usually yellow with black markings. They alert you to conditions that are immediately ahead. This sign indicates that there is a steep hill ahead. Slow down and be ready to shift to a lower gear to control your speed and protect your brakes from damage.

The question 21. If you are involved in a traffic accident in California, you must file a report of the accident with the DMV when:

1. The collision causes $1,000 in damage.
2. You plan on being out of the state for more than 30 days.
3. You refinance the remaining balance of your vehicle loan.

The correct answer is 1.

If a collision results in death, any minor or major injury, or more than $1,000 in damage to anyone's property, each driver involved must file a report with the DMV within 10 days. In some cases, the driver's insurance agent, broker, or legal representative may file the report to represent the driver.

The question 22. You are about to make a left turn. You must signal continuously during the last _____ feet before the turn.

1. 50
2. 75
3. 100

HILL

The correct answer is 3.

When making a left turn, you should begin signaling 100 feet before beginning the turn.

the question 23. Temporary signs used in construction and maintenance work areas:

1. Have a red background with green writing.
2. Have an orange background with black writing.
3. Have a yellow background with blue writing.

The correct answer is 2.

All temporary signs in work zones have orange backgrounds with black writing and/or symbols.

the question 24. You are driving on a freeway with a posted speed limit of 65 mph. Traffic is heavy and moving at 35 mph. The best speed for your vehicle is most likely:

1. 25 mph.
2. 35 mph.
3. 30 mph.

The correct answer is 2.

Collisions are more likely to happen when one driver travels more quickly or more slowly than the other vehicles on the road. You should enter a freeway at or near the speed of traffic, unless the speed of traffic exceeds the legal speed limit.

the question 25. Collisions are more likely to happen when:

1. All vehicles are traveling at about the same speed.
2. One lane of traffic is traveling faster than the other lanes.
3. One vehicle is traveling faster or slower than the flow of traffic.

The correct answer is 3.

Collisions are more likely to happen when one driver moves faster or slower than the other vehicles on the road. Driving faster than other traffic increases your chance of being involved in a collision. Driving more slowly than other traffic is also dangerous because it can increase the risk of a rear-end collision with your vehicle or cause other drivers to swerve to avoid hitting you.

the question 26. Driving under the influence of any medication which impairs your driving is permitted:

1. Under no circumstances.
2. If you don't feel drowsy.
3. If it is prescribed by a physician.

The correct answer is 1.

It is illegal to drive under the influence of any substance that impairs your ability to drive safely. This includes alcohol, prescription medications, over-the-counter medications, and illegal drugs.

the question 27. When double solid yellow lines separate lanes of traffic:

1. Passing is permitted from the left.
2. Passing is permitted from the right.
3. Passing is not permitted from either direction.

The correct answer is 3.

Yellow lines separating lanes of traffic indicate that traffic is moving in opposite directions. Double solid lines indicate that passing is not permitted from either direction.

the question 28. Drivers are required to obey instructions from:

1. Security guards patrolling parking lots.
2. Other drivers whose vehicles are broken down on the roadway.
3. Flaggers (signal persons) at construction sites.

The correct answer is 3.

Drivers must obey special signs or instructions given by flaggers. They are in place to keep drivers and workers safe.

the question 29. A school bus is stopped ahead of you in your lane with its red lights flashing. You should:

1. Stop and proceed when you think all of the children have exited the bus.
2. Slow to 25 mph and pass cautiously.
3. Stop for as long as the red lights are flashing.

The correct answer is 3.

When a stopped school bus is using its flashing red lights, approaching drivers must stop and remain stopped until the lights stop flashing. If the school bus is on the opposite side of a divided highway, drivers do not need to stop.

the question 30. If your car becomes disabled while on the highway, you should:

1. Stop in the right lane.
2. Park with all four wheels off the traveled highway, if possible.
3. Stop where you are.

The correct answer is 2.

f your vehicle becomes disabled, you must (if possible) park with all four wheels off of the main-traveled portion of the oad.

the question 31. What does this road sign indicate?

1. Directions for children
2. School zone ahead
3. Playground area ahead

the question 32. This sign means:

1. No U-turn.
2. Traffic signal ahead.
3. Railroad ahead.

The question 33. You enter a designated turn lane to make a left turn at an upcoming intersection. There is oncoming traffic. You should:

1. Move to the left of the center lane.
2. Signal before you arrive at the intersection.
3. Turn your front wheels to the left to be prepared to turn.

The correct answer is 2.
When making a left turn, you should always begin signaling about 100 feet before the turn. You should keep your front wheels aiming straight ahead until it is safe to start your turn. This ensures that you will not be pushed into oncoming traffic if another vehicle hits you from behind.

The question 34. You may make a left turn on a red light only from a:

1. One-way street onto a two-way street.
2. One-way street onto a one-way street.
3. Two-way street onto a one-way street.

The correct answer is 2.
A left turn against a red light can only be made from a one-way street onto a one-way street. Signal and stop for a red traffic light at the marked limit line.

the question 35. If you have a green light but traffic is blocking the intersection, you should:

1. Stay out of the intersection until traffic clears.
2. Enter the intersection and wait until traffic clears.
3. Merge into another lane and try to go around the traffic.

The correct answer is 1.

Even if your traffic light is green, you must not enter an intersection unless you can get completely across the intersection before the light turns red. If you block the intersection, you can be cited.

the question 36. If you are being passed in a no passing zone, you should:

1. Pull off the road.
2. Maintain your speed and position.
3. Slow down and let the other driver safely return to the drive lane.

The correct answer is 3.

Passing areas are based on how far ahead drivers can see.

Allow the passing vehicle to re-enter the drive lane as easily as possible to help everyone avoid potential upcoming hazards.

CALIFORNIA DMV Written TEST #12

the question 1. When driving in fog, it is best to drive with:

1. High beam headlights.
2. Low beam headlights.
3. Four-way flashers.

The correct answer is 2.

Use your low beam headlights when driving in fog, rain, or snow. High beam lights can reflect off the weather conditions, lowering visibility even more.

the question 2. If you hit an animal with your vehicle while driving on a California highway, you should:

1. Move the injured animal off the road.
2. Call the humane society.
3. Continue driving.

The correct answer is 2.

If you injure or kill an animal on the roadway, you should call CHP, the nearest humane society, or the police. You should not leave the animal to die or try to move the animal.

the question 3. Streets and highways are most slippery:

1. When it has been raining hard for several hours.
2. When they are clean and dry.
3. Just after it starts to rain.

The correct answer is 3.

Driving during the first half hour of rainfall is dangerous because roadways become extremely slippery when the water mixes with oil and other chemicals on the road surfaces that have not yet washed away. Use extra caution when driving on slippery roads.

the question 4. If your wheels drop off the roadway or pavement edge, you should:

1. Wait until it is safe to do so, then gradually re-enter the roadway.
2. Turn back onto the roadway immediately.
3. Stop.

The correct answer is 1.

If your wheels drop off the roadway or pavement edge, do not attempt to turn back onto the roadway immediately. Instead, reduce your speed, check traffic, and gradually turn back onto the roadway when it is safe to do so.

the question 5. As you enter into a roundabout, you should slow down and:

1. Yield to any crossing pedestrians and bicyclists.
2. Yield to any car already within the roundabout.
3. Both of the above.

The correct answer is 3.

When entering a roundabout, you must yield to pedestrians, bicyclists, and traffic already in the roundabout.

the question 6. You are driving on a freeway with a posted speed limit of 65 mph. Traffic is traveling at 70 mph. You may legally drive:

1. 70 mph or faster to keep up with the speed of traffi
2. Between 65 mph and 70 mph.
3. No faster than 65 mph.

The correct answer is 3.

On most California highways, the maximum speed limit is 65 mph. You may drive at 70 mph only if the speed limit is posted as such.

the question 7. When crossing a sidewalk to enter traffic from an alley or driveway, drivers should:

1. Stop only if pedestrians are on the sidewalk.
2. Stop before driving onto the sidewalk or sidewalk area.
3. Expect pedestrians on the sidewalk to yield the right-of-way.

The correct answer is 2.
When leaving an alley, driveway, or parking lot to enter a roadway, you must stop before driving onto a sidewalk or sidewalk area. Pedestrians and existing traffic have the right-of-way.

the question 8. If you are riding in a vehicle equipped with a lap belt and a separate shoulder belt, you are:

1. Only required to use the lap belt.
2. Required to use both the lap and shoulder belts.
3. Only required to use the shoulder belt.

The correct answer is 2.
If your vehicle is equipped with a lap belt and a separate shoulder belt, you are required to use both.

the question 9. Pedestrians crossing at corners have the right-of-way:

1. Only at controlled intersections.
2. Only when a crosswalk is painted on the street.
3. Whether or not a crosswalk is marked.

The correct answer is 3.

Respect the right-of-way of pedestrians. Always stop for any pedestrian crossing at a corner or crosswalk, even if the corner is without traffic signal lights. You should stop for pedestrians crossing at any crosswalk, whether or not the crosswalk is marked by painted lines.

the question 10. If your car begins to skid out of control, you should:

1. Pump the brakes.
2. Apply the brakes lightly.
3. Stay off the brakes.

The correct answer is 2.

If your vehicle is equipped with a lap belt and a separate shoulder belt, you are required to use both.

the question 11. You are involved in a minor collision at an intersection. There are no injuries and there is very little vehicle damage. You should:

1. Leave your vehicle in the traffic lane until law enforcement arrives.
2. Move your vehicle out of the traffic lane, if possible.
3. Not move your vehicle for any reason.

The correct answer is 2.

After a collision, if no one has been injured or killed and you can safely do so, you should move your vehicle out of the traffic lane.

the question 12. This road sign means:

1. No right turn.
2. Drive only in the direction of the arrow.
3. Curve ahead.

The correct answer is 2.

Regulatory signs provide notice to road users of traffic laws that must be obeyed. Where this sign is present, drivers must drive in the direction indicated by the arrow.

the question 13. When passing, you should move back into the right lane when:

1. You are one vehicle length ahead of the passed vehicle.
2. You can see both headlights of the passed vehicle in your rearview mirror.
3. You are 50 feet ahead of the passed vehicle.

The correct answer is 2.

Do not pass unless you have enough space to return to the driving lane. Before you return to the driving lane, be sure you have enough room between yourself and the vehicle you have passed. When you can see both headlights of the passed vehicle in your rearview mirror, it is safe to return to the driving lane.

the question 14. This sign is used to warn drivers that:

1. The right lane is ending and traffic should merge left.
2. The road curves ahead.
3. There are upcoming intersections.

The correct answer is 1.

Warning signs are usually yellow with black markings. They alert you to conditions that are immediately ahead. This sign warns drivers that the number of lanes is reduced ahead and that traffic should merge left.

the question 15. This sign means:

1. Upcoming downgrade or hill.
2. Road construction area.
3. Upcoming narrowing of roadway.

The correct answer is 1.
This sign warns of a dangerous downgrade or hill ahead.
The hill may be very long or steep, or it may have sharp
curves.

the question 16. When driving under low-visibility
conditions due to fog, you should:

1. Turn on your high beam headlights.
2. Slow down and use your low beam headlights.
3. Increase your speed so you do not cause
an accident.

The correct answer is 2.

When driving in fog, you should slow down and use your
low beam lights. If the fog is so dense that you cannot see,
pull off the road and wait for the fog to clear.

the question 17. Double solid yellow lane markings mean that:

1. Neither lane may pass.
2. Both lanes may pass.
3. The lane to the right may pass.

The correct answer is 1.

Yellow lane markings indicate a separation of lanes where traffic is traveling in opposite directions. When you see double solid yellow lane markings, passing is prohibited from both directions.

the question 18. If the driver of an oncoming vehicle fails to dim their headlights:

1. Look toward the center of the roadway.
2. Look toward the right side of the road.
3. Look straight ahead.

The correct answer is 2.

If an oncoming driver fails to dim their headlights, look toward the right side of the road. This will keep you from being blinded by the other vehicle's headlights and allow you to see enough of the road to stay on course. Do not try to retaliate by keeping your bright lights on.

the question 19. The speed limit on a school zone where children are present is _____, unless otherwise posted.

1. 15 mph
2. 25 mph
3. 20 mph

The correct answer is 2.

When driving within 500 to 1,000 feet of a school while children are outside or crossing the street, the speed limit is 25 mph, unless otherwise posted. Some school zones may have speed limits as low as 15 mph.

the question 20. Allow extra space in front of your vehicle when following a:

1. Station wagon.
2. Passenger vehicle.
3. Motorcycle.

The correct answer is 3.

Allow for extra space when driving behind a motorcycle. Motorcycles can stop more quickly than other vehicles can and you must have adequate room to stop if the motorcyclist brakes or falls off. Also, remember that motorcycles are difficult to see at night because they only have one tail light.

the question 21. When should you yield your legal right-of-way?

1. Often, even at controlled intersections.
2. Whenever it helps prevent collisions.
3. Never. It confuses other drivers.

The correct answer is 2.

Never assume other drivers will give you the right-of-way. Yield your right-of-way whenever it helps prevent collisions.

the question 22. A safety zone is a specially marked area for passengers to get on or off of buses or trolle· You may not drive through a safety zone:

1. When a bus or trolley is present.
2. When a bus or trolley is unloading passengers.
3. At any time for any reason.

The correct answer is 3.

You may never drive through a safety zone. This space is set aside for pedestrians.

the question 23. At a crosswalk:

1. You must yield to pedestrians.
2. Pedestrians must yield to you.
3. Construction workers must yield to you.

The correct answer is 1.

Pedestrians have the right-of-way at street crossings but must obey traffic control signals. Where a traffic signal is not present, vehicles must stop for pedestrians in a crosswalk, whether it is marked or unmarked.

the question 24. Various traffic control devices in construction and maintenance work areas are the color:

1. Red.
2. Orange.
3. Yellow.

The correct answer is 2.

Orange warning signs are used in and around work zones. Use special caution when you see orange signs, cones, or barriers on a roadway.

the question 25. The best thing to do if you become tired while driving is to:

1. Stop to rest or change drivers.
2. Drink coffee.
3. Open a window.

The correct answer is 1.

If you become tired while driving, it is best to stop to rest or change drivers. Being tired dulls your mind and slows down your reactions, making driving hazardous.

the question 26. A curb painted red means:

1. Loading zone.
2. The area is reserved for picking up or dropping off passengers.
3. No parking, standing, or stopping.

The correct answer is 3.

You may not stop, stand, or park at a red-painted curb.

the question 27. When is it legal for minors to use a cell phone without a hands-free device while driving?

1. When making a call while stopped at the red light
2. When making a call for emergency assistance
3. Never

The correct answer is 2.

It is illegal for minors to use a cell phone at all while driving, except to contact an emergency entity in an emergency situation. For adult drivers, the use of hands-free devices is permitted; however, to avoid distractions, it is advisable to make calls only if needed to call for help in an emergency.

the question 28. Abandoning an animal on the highway may result in:

1. Jail time.
2. A point against your license.
3. No legal consequences.

The correct answer is 1.

It is illegal to dump or abandon an animal on the highway. Doing so can result in six months of jail time, a fine of up to $1,000, or both.

the question 29. Make room for cars that are entering the freeway by:

1. Slowing down.
2. Merging into a different lane.
3. Maintaining your speed and position.

The correct answer is 2.

Make room for vehicles that are entering a freeway. If possible, merge into the next lane to create a gap for the incoming vehicles. If you cannot merge, adjust your speed to allow for the vehicles to enter traffic as smoothly and safely as possible.

the question 30. If a traffic signal light is green and a police officer signals for you to stop, you should:

1. Obey the officer.
2. Obey the traffic signal.
3. Do what the vehicle in front of you does.

The correct answer is 1.

Drivers must obey any instructions given by a police officer, even if the instructions contradict laws, signs, signals, or markings that would otherwise apply.

The question 31. You may legally block an intersection:

1. If you entered the intersection on the green light.
2. During rush hour traffic.
3. Under no circumstances.

The correct answer is 3.
Even if the light is green, you may not enter an intersection unless you can get completely across before the light turns red. If you block the intersection, you can be cited.

The question 32. You are getting ready to make a right turn. You should:

1. Signal and turn immediately.
2. Stop before entering the right lane and let all other traffic go first.
3. Slow down or stop, if necessary, and then make the turn.

The correct answer is 3.
When making a right turn, you should begin signaling about 100 feet before the turn, reduce your speed, stop behind the limit line (if applicable), and then make the turn.

the question 33. To avoid last-minute moves, you should be looking down the road to where your vehicle will be in about:

1. 5 to 10 seconds.
2. 10 to 15 seconds.
3. 15 to 20 seconds.

The correct answer is 2.

To avoid last-minute moves, you should scan the road 10 to 15 seconds ahead of your vehicle. This allows you to see hazards before meeting them.

the question 34. When you see an emergency vehicle approaching while using its flashing lights, you must:

1. Maintain your speed and stay in your lane until the vehicle has passed.
2. Move into the right lane and drive slowly until the vehicle has passed.
3. Pull over to the curb or edge of the road and stop until the vehicle has passed.

The correct answer is 3.

If you see an emergency vehicle approaching while using its flashing lights, pull over to the right edge of the road and stop. Position yourself parallel to the curb. On one-way streets, drive toward the road edge nearest you.

the question 35. All of the following are dangerous to do while driving. Which is also illegal?

1. Wearing a headset that covers both ears
2. Having one or more interior lights on
3. Using cruise control on residential streets

The correct answer is 1.

Do not wear a headset or earplugs in both ears while driving; it is against the law. You must be able to be aware of all possible surrounding hazards.

the question 36. Three of the most important times to check for traffic behind you are before:

1. Backing, making a sharp turn, or crossing an intersection.
2. Backing, changing lanes, or slowing down quickly.
3. Changing lanes, crossing intersections, or slowing down quickly.

The correct answer is 2.

It is important to check behind you before changing lanes, reducing your speed, backing up, or driving down a long or steep hill.

DMV_Driving_Test

DMV Driving Test

Made in the USA
Las Vegas, NV
22 October 2023